The Public Relations Writer's Handbook

From pitches and press releases to news and feature stories, to social media writing and more, this new book by author Whitney Lehmann and a handful of experienced contributors breaks down the most widely used types of public relations writing needed to become a PR pro.

The Public Relations Writer's Handbook serves as a guide for those both in the classroom and in the field who want to learn, and master, the style and techniques of public relations writing. Eighteen conversational chapters provide an overview of the most popular forms of public relations writing, focusing on media relations, storytelling, writing for the web/social media, business and executive communications, event planning and more. Chapters include user-friendly writing templates, exercises and AP Style skill drills and training.

Whether you're a PR major or PR practitioner, this book is for you. Lehmann has combined her industry and classroom experience to create a handbook that's accessible for PR students and practitioners alike.

A dedicated eResource also supports the book, with writing templates and answer keys (for instructors) to the end-of-chapter exercises in the text.

Whitney Lehmann, Ph.D., APR, is an assistant professor of communication in the Department of Writing and Communication at Nova Southeastern University, USA. Her industry experience includes working for Seminole Hard Rock Hotel & Casino, Miami International Airport, Barry University and the *Miami Herald*.

The Public Relations Writer's Handbook

Whitney Lehmann, Ph.D., APR

Routledge
Taylor & Francis Group

NEW YORK AND LONDON

First published 2020
by Routledge
52 Vanderbilt Avenue, New York, NY 10017

and by Routledge
2 Park Square, Milton Park, Abingdon, Oxon, OX14 4RN

Routledge is an imprint of the Taylor & Francis Group, an informa business

Library of Congress Cataloging-in-Publication Data
A catalog record for this title has been requested

ISBN: 978-0-8153-6529-7 (hbk)
ISBN: 978-0-8153-6528-0 (pbk)
ISBN: 978-1-351-26192-0 (ebk)

Typeset in Gill
by Newgen Publishing UK

Visit the eResources: https://www.routledge.com/product/9780815365280

To Michael Laderman,

My first boss, lifelong mentor and cherished friend.

For giving me my start in this field, sharing your passion for it and guiding me at every turn.

Contents

Contributors

Heidi Carr is a lecturer at the University of Miami's School of Communication. Her favorite topics to teach include Writing for PR, Media Relations, Pitching and specialized courses focused on Politics, Travel and Tourism and Gender Messaging. She is also the academic adviser for the university's Public Relations Student Society of America. Carr joined the faculty full time in 2013 after a 25-year career as a journalist. Most of that was at the *Miami Herald*, where she worked as the night city editor, bureau editor and copy editor. The Virginia native earned her Bachelor of Arts from the College of William and Mary, and a Master of Science from the Medill School of Journalism at Northwestern University.

Lawrence Carrino has over 20 years of experience at an industry leading, culinary & tourism communications agency, Brustman Carrino Public Relations. President Larry Carrino is highly revered in the Magic City. In 2009, he was selected as one of the Top "40 Under 40" Professionals by *Gold Coast* magazine and was cited as "Best Flack" by *Miami New Times* in 2008 and again in 2013. He was honored in 2015 with a *South Florida Business Journal's* Miami Ultimate CEO Award and, in 2019, received a Johnson & Wales University ZEST Award for Character and was inducted into *BIZBASH* Florida's Hall of Fame. He currently spearheads regional PR efforts for the famed *Food Network & Cooking Channel South Beach Wine & Food Festival* and maintains the role of PR chair for Slow Food Miami.

Kimberly Cohane is an award-winning higher education digital and social media marketing professional with extensive experience in digital campaigns and social media. She worked as an online marketing and social media professional for over 10 years at Nova Southeastern University (NSU). During this time, she led innovative ways to amplify NSU's brand through a multi-tiered strategy including digital advertising, Pay Per Click (PPC) ads, social media and virtual reality (VR) tours. She is currently a graduate intern for the U.S. Department of State and a Ph.D. candidate for Conflict Analysis and Resolution at NSU researching how social media bots disrupt online communities.

Megan Fitzgerald Dunn, Ph.D., an associate professor at Nova Southeastern University, earned her Ph.D. in communication from Florida State University, her M.A. in journalism from Syracuse University and her B.A. in communication from Stonehill College. She teaches a variety of communication and journalism courses, including media regulation, multimedia writing and public speaking. She also serves as the faculty adviser for the university's student-run newspaper, *The Current*.

Virginia Gil is the Miami editor and Markets editor-at-large for *Time Out*. She covers eating, drinking and going out in Miami — plus everything else there is to see and do in the 305. Whether it's discovering a new restaurant, uncovering a fresh cocktail trend or getting the scoop on an underground concert, she has the intel you need to make the most of your Miami experience. Virginia studied at the University of Miami, worked as an editor at local lifestyle publications — *Daily Candy, MIAMI Magazine*, and many others — and has spent the last 15 years writing about food and drink in both Miami and New York. Eating, drinking and writing are her passions — in that order. As a born-and-bred Miami girl, her cravings for croquetas are discerning and her hair is impermeable to humidity.

Jeremy Katzman serves as Director of Business Development for Nova Southeastern University and is part of the Health Professions Division's leadership team. He is also senior adviser to the Dean and formerly served as Director of Public Relations and Marketing for the NSU Dr. Kiran C. Patel College of Allopathic Medicine. He has held various communications roles with organizations such as Miami Children's Hospital Foundation, Mednax and O'Connell & Goldberg Public Relations. Katzman was named 2018 Communicator of the Year by the Public Relations Society of America (PRSA) Greater Fort Lauderdale Chapter. He is accredited in public relations (APR) by the Universal Accreditation Board. He earned his M.B.A. from Nova Southeastern University and holds a B.A. in public relations and a B.S. in political science from the University of Florida (UF). He is a member of the UF Hall of Fame.

Michael Laderman is an Orlando-based award-winning writer, public affairs, marketing, advertising and brand management executive. He has led the public and media relations efforts of the Orlando Museum of Art, Nova Southeastern University and Barry University, and directed all executive communications for Clemson University. Throughout his career, Laderman has also had the opportunity to represent such individuals as Shaquille O'Neal, world-renowned saxophone player "Mr. Casual" Charlie DeChant, and Haiti's Prime Minister Laurent Lamothe, to name just a few of the many celebrities he has worked with and alongside. He is the founder and executive director of 20 A-M COMMUNICATIONS, Share My Story and The Share My Story Foundation, Inc., and proudly serves the community as a member of the Florida Association of Veteran Owned Businesses and the Healthcare Industry Networking Team of Florida.

Merrie Meyers, Ph.D., APR, Fellow PRSA practiced public relations in the public and private sector. She was a journalist, newspaper executive and briefly worked in financial public relations. During 25 years in education public relations she managed responses to issues in health, safety and national disasters that garnered national recognition. Her business-education partnerships generated $5 million in donations. As a college grant writer, proposals she authored secured $40 million. Meyers has undergraduate and graduate degrees from the University of Florida, and a Ph.D. from Florida Atlantic University. She is an adjunct instructor, newsmagazine editor and non-profit volunteer.

Michael North, Ph.D., teaches public relations writing and social media as an assistant professor at Central Connecticut State University. He earned his Ph.D. in mass communication at the University of Miami where he focused his research on how Fortune 500 companies use social media to communicate with stakeholders. North's research focuses primarily on social media with specific attention paid to Twitter. His research interests center on how companies communicate with their stakeholders and what value these companies can derive from social media.

Foreword

The irony of writing this textbook's Foreword is not lost on me.

For years, when speaking to college classes — either my own when teaching a summer media relations course at Barry University or as a guest speaker and presenter for others — I would typically begin with the following warning: Whatever you have read in a college textbook re: communications, public and media relations, marketing, etc., take it with a grain of salt.

I would state that, due to my complete disbelief of text that is typically written in a way that makes it seem as though there is just one way to do public relations — those being the ways of the respective author whose book was held in hand at that time.

My career, and the successes that have come with it, have been courtesy of my studies within the College of Life and the University of Experience. Whereas I earned an associate's degree in journalism and a bachelor's in humanities, my abilities to successfully oversee million-dollar campaigns for universities came through via the overall understanding and admittance of the following:

> This is a completely subjective field, and marketing research technically tells you nothing.

Research typically states what just happened, not what *will* happen. It does not tell you what a prospective student — looking into universities to see which one they will attend — will do when they receive your promotional email and your brochure and your letter. It will not tell you how they will like it. It will not tell you how they will respond to it.

So it is that subjective understanding — that no set amount of research and education and studying can ever guarantee results, and as such, there is no one set way to do public relations, marketing, advertising, brand management — that led to my mantra which has lasted me more than 30 years in this business as told to more than 50 direct employees and then some:

> Be yourself and do the little things

Meaning: Don't act like a salesperson and proactively go above-and-beyond the basics that only get you so far in life. Do those things that should be expected but aren't, that most people don't do, in a way that is truly yours.

Of all employees that I ever had the pleasure of directing, Whitney Lehmann, Ph.D., did those things better than any other.

And in an interview process that entailed more than 200 applicants for the communications coordinator position that she originally applied for, do you know how she even got an interview?

Her writing style ... that included a cover letter that read as though she was speaking personally to me in the same room, and a resume that flowed, sans canned words and phrases.

Her written words made her stand out among the others, enough to get an interview with me. Her in-person attitude and demeanor — displaying the details of one who was clearly herself [e.g. not forcing a fake "interview persona" on me], who shared a "team-first" mentality — got her the job.

Did she have the best resume, and was she the most qualified? Probably, and most likely, not. But she stood out.

Whitney Lehmann ended up being one of, if not THE, best hires I ever made.

She is one who knew instantly how to be herself, and she was extremely willing to do those little things that sets you apart in this business. A former journalist, she would call reporters back right away. She knew how to talk with deans and faculty and administrators. She knew how to meet a deadline. She knew how to be polite. She knew how to work extra hours. She knew that all of that came with this business, and in this industry.

Those are the little things that I spoke of before. And, in doing those little things, that was her just being herself.

Now, though, let's go back to what really helped her stand apart. Did you catch it? Did you notice it? It wasn't just her attitude. It wasn't just her willingness to work hard.

It was her writing skill. It was the talent that she had to turn a simple cover letter into a story. It was the skill set that she had, which made her — and her resume — stand out, all because of how well it was written.

Without that skillset — the talent of taking words and actually knowing how to use them in various forms and ways — I never would have wanted to meet her. I never would have wanted to learn more about her. I never would have wanted to interview her.

When she wrote her cover letter and resume, when she submitted them to me, she didn't know the precise kind of human being I was looking for in filling that specific position. She had no way of knowing that I was wanting the candidate who, I subjectively felt, was the best overall person with the best overall attitude for the job. She had no way of knowing that, even with those human-based skills, had she not have had the talent to write as she did, she would have been just another candidate in the delete bin.

Her words, though, set her apart. How she *wrote* her words set her apart.

It is a total combination of things that you must need to have happen in order to gain your first job, and your second job and your third job and then some.

That is the importance of writing. Understanding that the written word can, and potentially will, take you on journeys that can entail a new career in public relations, social and traditional communications, and beyond.

You know, when I first met Whitney Lehmann, the world of social media was just beginning to grow. Side-by-side, we not only adapted to it, but we helped set the standards for it. And all along, whether it was Facebook or Twitter or LinkedIn, etc., one constant remained: You had to know how to write, and you had to know how to tell a story. You had to know how to write a full sentence. You had to know how to write a feature. You had to know how to write news. And you had to make it all flow.

And if you didn't, it didn't matter the kind of person you were or the little things that you did to succeed. As a communicator in this field, you had to have the total package. You had to understand the importance of writing, not just the importance of being yourself and doing the little things.

What makes this book, and its author, so special and so unique is that Whitney Lehmann understands it better than any other colleague that I have ever met. She has always, and naturally, understood those concepts and that mantra.

Within the pages that follow throughout this textbook, you will learn through Whitney Lehmann how to write within the world of public relations, marketing, advertising, social and traditional media, etc. But just as important, and more specifically, keep an eye out for *how* Whitney Lehmann writes this book. Keep an eye out for the style that she uses. Because her style that she uses is one that she used for years as a member of my team.

It is what makes her *her*, as herself. It will be as though she is with you, talking to you, directly teaching you the aspects of the business that we do.

Understand the meaning when I say the following: Listen hard while reading her words.

And then be yourself and do the little things.

Michael Laderman

Preface

As we enter this new decade, public relations practitioners are expected to be many things: writers, editors, reporters, social media strategists, event coordinators, public speakers, image consultants, communications coaches, crisis communicators, fact checkers, branding experts, photographers, videographers, directors, media wranglers, relationship builders and storytellers.

In essence, we are communication ninjas.

During the last decade, I've had the extraordinary opportunity to try on many of these different hats. I've stood on the National Mall in a sea of millions of Americans, reporting on the day that our first African American president took office; tweeted minute-by-minute updates to scared and frustrated airport customers who were stuck mid-air in a skytrain during a lightning storm; written a last-minute script for a celebrity chef moments before he stepped on stage; coached clients through stressful, live TV segments; developed a digital media kit for a national, star-studded food festival; crafted the copy for a customer-driven app for a client's nearly 1 million weekly visitors; and most recently, launched a Generation Z-focused social media program for a client wanting to connect with its social-savvy, Snapchat-loving audience.

The hats we wear as public relations practitioners will continue to evolve and change; however, the goal will always remain the same: to communicate clearly, concisely, honestly, objectively and persuasively, while ensuring that communication is two-way, mutually beneficial and sensitive to all types of diversity. Whether we're preparing speaking points, issuing a media alert, drafting a press release, tweeting breaking news, writing photo captions, pitching to the media, editing a bio, piecing together a policy or anything else, public relations writing is truly at the heart of everything we do.

As the field of public relations continues to grow globally, it's imperative that public relations practitioners around the world are equipped with the proper tools and training they need to meet the demands of this ever-evolving industry. I am a firm believer that if someone can learn to communicate well, both in the spoken and written word, they can accomplish just about anything.

In this text, I focus on the written word from a public relations perspective. I've drawn from my time in the field to boil this book down to the public relations writing essentials, including media relations, storytelling, writing for the web/social media, business and executive communications, event planning, and more. Each chapter includes user-friendly writing templates that will have you mastering the content, and the art of PR writing, in no time.

To give you multiple perspectives, I've also included input from real-world PR professionals, all of whom I've had the privilege and pleasure of working with or for during my career. These PR pros have contributed chapters and shared their personal experience working with various forms of PR writing in features called "Perspective from the Pros."

For those of you tasked with being PR writing educators, I've got your back, too. I've included a digital copy of each template and assignment (for use with Canvas, Blackboard and other learning management systems), as well as answer keys to help keep grading effortless and consistent.

Whether you're new to public relations or already a PR pro, I hope this text ignites your passion for the field and the future you can have in it. Now, it's time to get your PR ninja on!

Acknowledgments

My journey in the field of public relations, including the writing of this text, would not have been possible without the assistance of the following people:

Mike Laderman, to whom I am forever indebted for giving me my start in, and passion for, public relations. Thank you for taking a chance on me, for helping me develop as a writer, for teaching me the principles of public relations, and for serving as a guiding force throughout my career ... and, of course, for lending your infinite industry knowledge and talents to this text. I can never thank you enough.

To Routledge, for the tremendous opportunity, and to Felisa Salvago-Keyes, for your professionalism, publishing expertise and patience with this new mom as she navigates the work/baby balance. Thank you for making the publishing process a pleasure.

The contributors of this text — Heidi Carr, Larry Carrino, Kim Cohane, Dr. Megan Fitzgerald, Virginia Gil, Jeremy Katzman, Mike Laderman, Dr. Merrie Meyers and Dr. Mike North — for lending your time, talents and extensive experience and for being my "go-to" people in the field. The knowledge and perspective that you've brought to this text are invaluable.

Dr. Mitchell Shaprio, my dissertation chair and respected mentor, for making my dream of becoming a communication faculty member a reality and for helping me navigate this next chapter now that I'm here. Without you, none of this would have been possible.

Palma Leonatti, for giving me the PR experience of a lifetime at Seminole Hard Rock Hollywood. Working for you, with you and with the Seminole Hard Rock Hollywood team will always be one of the most amazing and exciting experiences of my career. Thank you for your friendship, your mentorship and for the many, many laughs we shared working together. You will always be my Gemini soul sister.

Dr. Alyse Lancaster for giving me the opportunity as a doctoral student to teach Public Relations Writing for the University of Miami's Department of Strategic Communication. Teaching this course will always be the highlight of my time as a doctoral student. Thank you for the privilege.

The PR professors at the University of Miami — Heidi Carr, Dr. Maria Scott, Dr. Colee Splichal, Randy Stano and Dr. Don Tilson — who graciously allowed me to shadow them in their PR courses. You still set the standard for my own teaching today.

Dr. Shanti Bruce for giving me a second home as a faculty member in the Department of Writing and Communication within NSU's College of Arts, Humanities, and Social Sciences. Your leadership inspires me, motivates me, challenges me and empowers me to be the best version of myself — both personally and professionally. Thank you for making me a part of the team.

Dr. Claire Lutkewitte, who was instrumental in helping me get this book to fruition. For taking the time to mentor a junior faculty member and helping me navigate the publishing process. Thank you for your friendship and for selflessly sharing your knowledge and experience.

My best friend, Nicole Farruggia, who teaches me and inspires me to be a stronger communicator every single day.

My parents, Linda and Gary, my in-laws, Sharon and Pete, and my siblings, Johnny and Brooke, for your constant support and your endless hours of babysitting that made this project possible.

My loving, handsome husband and biggest cheerleader, Colton. Your unconditional love gives me the ability to fearlessly chase my dreams, including this one.

My son, Charleston Taylor. Being your mom will always be my favorite job of all.

My students — past, present and future — for inspiring me daily and for sharing this lifelong love of PR with me. May this book inspire you to be the best PR professionals possible.

Finally, but always first, God. Doing your work will always be the most important work that I can ever do.

What Is Public Relations Writing?

Chapter 1

Purpose, Process, Style, Form and Tone

Whitney Lehmann

Purpose

What is Public Relations?

What is public relations writing and what makes it different from other types of writing? Before we dive into defining PR writing, we must first define the term public relations.

Public relations is defined by various texts and authors in a multitude of ways:

- "Executives increasingly see public relations not as publicity and one-way communication, but as a complex and dynamic process of negotiation and compromise with a number of key audiences, which are often called 'publics'" (Wilcox, Cameron & Reber, 2016, p. 67).
- "Public relations is the management function that establishes and maintains mutually beneficial relationships between an organization and the publics on whom its success or failure depends" (Broom & Sha, 2013, p. 5).
- "You can grasp the essential elements of effective public relations by remembering the following words and phrases: deliberate ... planned ... performance ... public interest ... two-way communication ...strategic management function" (Wilcox, Cameron & Reber, 2016, p. 7).
- "Public relations builds goodwill and an understanding of organizational goals among various internal and external publics to help the organization operate smoothly and conduct its business in a cooperative, conflict-free environment" (Zappala & Carden, 2010, p. 4).
- "In answering the question 'What is public relations?' we now know that public relations is (1) a management function that (2) conducts research about an organization *and* its publics to (3) establish mutually beneficial relationships through (4) communication" (Stacks, 2017, p. 19).
- "Public relations helps people see the good things about an organization, which is possible only when the organization actually is doing good things. Often public relations drives an organization's decisions to adapt and operate more for the public benefit" (Smith, 2017, p. 1).

The Public Relations Society of America (PRSA) and other public relations organizations around the world offer definitions that also emphasize terms such as "strategic," "management," "process," "publics," "mutually beneficial relationships," "goodwill" and "mutual understanding," among others.

- *Public Relations Society of America (PRSA):* "Public relations, as defined by PRSA, 'is a strategic communication process that builds mutually beneficial relationships between organizations and their publics.' At its core, public relations is about influencing, engaging and building a relationship with key stakeholders to contribute to the way an organization is perceived" (Learn About PR, 2019).
- *Canadian Public Relations Society (CPRS):* "Public relations is the strategic management of relationships between an organization and its diverse publics, through the use of communication, to achieve mutual understanding, realize organizational goals and serve the public interest" (About, 2008).
- *Public Relations Institute of Australia (PRIA):* "Public Relations is a management function involving effective communication between an organisation and the people and organisations that may be interested in, concerned about or need to know (i.e. should be told) how they may be affected by the activities or future plans of the organisation" (What is it?, 2019).
- *Chartered Institute of Public Relations (CIPR) in the United Kingdom:* "Public relations is the discipline which looks after reputation, with the aim of earning understanding and support and influencing opinion and behavior. It is the planned and sustained effort to establish and maintain goodwill and mutual understanding between an organisation and its publics" (About PR, n.d.).
- *Middle East Public Relations Association (MERPA):* "At MEPRA, we believe that public relations is a strategic discipline that focuses on reaching and influencing an organization's stakeholders. Because an organization's reputation is based on strong relationships with its stakeholders — employees, investors, the media, bloggers, government officials, to name a few — it is the responsibility of public relations to help build an organization's relationships in order to influence stakeholders' attitude, opinion, and ultimately their behavior."

In my classes, when introducing students to the term, I similarly define public relations as "building and maintaining mutually beneficial relationships" and as "managing the flow of information between an organization and its publics." I emphasize "publics," rather than "public," as the above definitions do, because an organization has many publics that it communicates with. A university, for example, has internal publics, such as students, faculty and staff, as well as external publics, such as prospective students, parents, alumni, donors, the local community, the media and others.

I like to think of the public relations practitioner as the "middle man" (or woman) who manages that two-way flow of communication. I also emphasize "two-way," because we, as PR practitioners do not simply speak *at* publics; we communicate *with* publics to facilitate communication that is mutually beneficial for both them and the client. "Public relations professionals promote two-way communication by providing an open flow of idea exchange, feedback and information between an organization and its publics" (Zappala & Carden, 2010, p. 4).

Public relations is *not* (Smith, 2017):

- hype or exaggeration
- about lying
- secretive
- about manipulating people
- about spin or deception
- only about publicity

The purpose of public relations is not to make the client look good but rather "simple words and clear messages that inspire a desired change in thinking or behavior" (Zappala & Carden, 2010, p. 4).

Public Relations vs. Marketing and Advertising

In defining public relations, it's also important to distinguish it from marketing and advertising, two disciplines it often gets confused with, because although all three work together and share the common goal of helping an organization communicate to its publics, each has its own distinct purpose. While public relations focuses on building relationships, creating goodwill, support and mutual understanding, marketing seeks an economic exchange using the four Ps (product, price, place and promotion) and advertising seeks to attract customers through paid, controlled messages.

In order to fully understand how public relations differs from and integrates with marketing and advertising, let's examine the main objectives of each discipline further.

Marketing

Marketing is transaction-oriented; it focuses on developing, maintaining and improving a product's market share, attracting customers and causing a transaction in order to build profitability (Zappala & Carden, 2010). Authors have also defined marketing in the following ways:

> The purpose of marketing is to sell goods and services through attractive packaging, competitive pricing, retail and online promotions, and effective distribution systems. (Wilcox, Cameron, & Reber, 2016, p. 14)

> Marketing is the management function that identifies human needs and wants, offers products and services to satisfy those demands, and causes transactions that deliver products and services to users in exchange for something of value to the provider. (Broom & Sha, 2013, p. 5)

While marketing seeks to increase market share in order to meet an organization's economic objectives, public relations is concerned with social capital; it seeks "to build relationships with a variety of publics that can enhance the organization's reputation and establish trust in its policies, products and services" (Wilcox, Cameron, & Reber, 2016, p. 14).

Advertising

Similar to marketing, *advertising* also has the goal of attracting customers but through paid promotional messages that can be controlled (Zappala & Carden, 2010).

> Advertising is information placed in the media by an identified sponsor that pays for the time or space. It is a controlled method of placing messages in the media.
> (Broom & Sha, 2013, p. 8)

> Broadly defined, advertising is persuasive communication through purchased media to promote a product, service, or idea on behalf of an identified organization or sponsor.
> (Smith, 2017, p. 12)

Publicity, one area of public relations, is *earned media*, meaning it wasn't paid for. "Editors, also known as gatekeepers, make the decision to use the material as a news item and the organization doesn't pay for the placement" (Wilcox, Cameron & Reber, 2016, p. 14).

Advertising, on the other hand, is *paid media*, which involves a contracted rate with a media outlet to buy space or time. "An organization writes the content, decides the type and graphics, and controls where and when the advertisement will be used" (Wilcox, Cameron & Reber, 2016, p. 14).

When advertisers pay for time or space, they have the ability to control the messaging; public relations practitioners, however, are at the mercy of the media. News organizations choose whether or not to use the information sent to them by PR professionals based on the information's news value. "Publicity is an uncontrolled method of placing messages because the source does not pay the media for placement and cannot guarantee if or how the material will be used" (Universal Accreditation Board, 2017, p. 19).

What is Public Relations Writing?

Now that we've defined public relations, we can begin to define *public relations writing* and its purpose — to communicate information that will influence people.

> Public relations writing succeeds when people respond by doing something your organization wants them to do, whether that be learning something you want them to learn, adopting an attitude or position you want them to adopt, taking a positive action you want them to take, or simply thinking good thoughts about the organization. In the public relations world, writing without such a purpose is a waste of time.
> (Zappala & Carden, 2010, p. 3)

Public relations writing is also strategic and targets specific publics.

It's important to distinguish the term "public" from the term "audience." Whereas a *public* represents a group of people brought together by some common factor or interest, an *audience* represents a group of listeners or viewers who may receive the same message but otherwise have no connection to one another (Universal Accreditation Board, 2017). Examples of publics targeted by public relations could be residents of a neighborhood, advocates of certain issues, fans of a sports team, or members of the media.

Finally, public relations writing takes many different forms, including:

- Media relations (e.g., news releases, media advisories/alerts, media pitches, public service announcements)
- Business and executive communications (e.g., speeches, memos, letters, company newsletters and magazines, annual reports)
- Internal communications (e.g., content for an organization's intranet, employee newsletters, training/orientation materials)
- Writing for digital media (e.g., email, content for websites, blogs and social media channels, video news releases, electronic media kits)
- Storytelling (e.g., backgrounders, fact sheets, bio sketches, news and feature stories, photo captions)
- Advocacy writing (e.g., letters to the editor, articles for opinion pages and other types of writing that establish a position or comment on an issue)
- Writing for events (e.g., talking points, shot lists, run-of-show)
- Crisis communications (e.g., crisis messaging for an organization to post to its website and social channels and/or send out via text or recorded message)
- Writing for controlled media (e.g., advertising copy, product brochures/promotions)
- And more.

A typical day on the job for a public relations professional, for example, could include: drafting an annual report for stakeholders; crafting a caption to engage social media followers; writing a news release for members of the media; scripting a speech for a CEO; editing an employee newsletter; publishing content to the company's website for customers; and much more.

It should be noted that while public relations is not synonymous with marketing or advertising, public relations professionals do often work with the marketing and advertising departments within their organizations to develop content for various marketing and advertising projects (e.g., product packaging, direct-mail pieces, customer newsletters, advertising copy, etc.). This type of public relations writing involves writing for controlled media (as stated above).

Media Relations

While certainly not the only public targeted by public relations professionals, the media are one of the most targeted publics of public relations writing. Much of public relations writing is directed at news organizations and members of the media, called *gatekeepers*, defined as "people or processes that filter information by deciding which content is published, broadcasted, posted, shared or forwarded" (Kelleher, 2018, p. 180). Gatekeepers include "reporters, editors, news directors, bloggers, and others who control access to the media" (Kelleher, 2018, p. 143).

The symbiotic relationship that PR practitioners have with journalists is referred to as *media relations* and is defined as "mutually beneficial associations between publicists or public relations professionals and journalists as a condition for reaching publics with messages of news or features of interest (publicity)" (Universal Accreditation Board, 2017, p. 18).

Public relations professionals need journalists and members of the media to "provide a vehicle to present the organization's messages" and reporters and editors need PR practitioners to "help them identify newsworthy stories and report on them" (Smith, 2017, p. 306).

Public relations writing shares many similarities with journalistic writing, including style (Associated Press Stylebook), form (inverted pyramid), tone (simple language that's straight to the point and sticks to the facts) and voice (mainly third-person point of view). We'll examine style, form, tone and voice further in this chapter. But first, let's examine the role that public relations writing plays in the public relations process.

Process

Now that we've looked at various definitions of public relations, we can begin to examine public relations writing, its purpose and key characteristics. In order to truly understand the purpose of public relations writing, we need to first understand where it falls within the *public relations process*.

The four-phase public relations process, as advocated by the Public Relations Society of America (PRSA), includes research, planning, implementation and evaluation and is often referred to as RPIE. It should be noted, however, that there are similar, accepted acronyms used for this process, such as RACE (Research and planning, Action, Communication, Evaluation), ROPE (Research, Objectives, Programming, Evaluation) and PIE (Planning, Implementation and Evaluation).

Regardless of the acronym used, the process used to guide any public relations plan should include the following (Study Guide for the Certificate in Principles of Public Relations Examination, 2015):

- Research/analysis of the situation
- Planning, goal/objective setting
- Implementation/execution/communication
- Evaluation

While there are many texts dedicated entirely to the art of the public relations process, my goal, for the purposes of introducing you to the art of public relations writing is help you understand where PR writing fits in this process.

Public relations writing falls within the Implementation phase. Once we've assessed the situation during the Research phase and set our goal/objectives during the Planning phase, we are ready to execute the plan and communicate during the Implementation phase.

It is in this phase — Implementation — where public relations writing lives. Our overarching goal, supporting objectives and strategies for the PR plan are carried out through tactics. *Tactics* are the "nuts-and-bolts part of the plan" and "describe the specific activities that put each strategy into operation and help to achieve the stated objectives" (Wilcox, Cameron & Reber, 2016, p. 112).

Whereas strategies typically refer to "the overall concept, approach, or general plan for the program designed to achieve an objective," tactics refer to "the actual events, media, and methods used to implement the strategy" (Broom & Sha, 2013, p. 273). Tactics are the most visible portion of a PR plan and "use various methods to reach target audiences with key messages" (Wilcox, Cameron & Reber, 2016, p. 112).

For example, if a stated objective within a PR plan is "to secure 10 media hits featuring the client's new product in national outlets by June 1," one strategy to achieve that objective may be developing a strategic media kit to promote the product. Tactics to support that strategy would include all the steps involved in developing the media kit, such as crafting a backgrounder detailing the organization's history and mission (Chapter 8), drafting bio sketches for its executives (Chapter 10), writing a timely news release about the product launch (Chapter 2), designing a fact sheet highlighting product information (Chapter 9), and creating a targeted media pitch inviting members of the media to attend the product launch, interview select executives and try the product first-hand (Chapter 3).

Public relations writing comes to life through tactics, but it is also so much more than simply writing a news release, crafting a social media caption or drafting talking points for an executive. It has a specific purpose, process, style, form and tone (hence, the title of this chapter).

When describing the purpose and process of public relations writing to my students, I like to use the analogy or a water filter pitcher — you know, the kind you keep in your fridge. You fill it with tap water, the water flows through the filter, the filter removes lead, chlorine, chemicals, heavy metals and other contaminants, and ultimately, produces purer, safer and better-tasting water.

Our job, as public relations practitioners, is to "filter," edit and organize the information we are presented with from the organization for the intended public. For example, when crafting a timely news release for the media regarding a recall issued by a toy manufacturer, a PR manager for the organization would first begin by interviewing one or several executives in order to gather pertinent information. Following the interview, he or she may have several pages of interview notes and would then edit this information down to the crucial information needed to craft the news release, including: the who, what, where, when, why and how; supporting quotes from key executives; and other relevant details, such as next steps for consumers affected by the recall, a phone number they can call with questions and a URL they can visit to learn more about the recall.

Primary and Secondary Research

Speaking of the interview process, let's back up for a moment to examine Research — the first phase — and how it has a close connection to public relations writing.

Before the writing can ever begin, public relations practitioners must analyze the situation using primary and secondary research. Public relations writers often start by conducting *secondary research* — existing information in books, news articles, electronic databases, etc. Secondary sources can include newspaper articles, magazine articles, blog posts, radio interviews, broadcast segments, newsletters, memos, archival records, reference books, fact sheets and other existing background materials, and more.

Once all existing information is gathered, public relations writers can identify any gaps in information and use these holes to design and conduct *primary research* — new and original information researchers collect directly through surveys, interviews, observations and other means.

We'll take an in-depth look at the interview process — a method of primary research that public relations writers use daily — in Chapter 7. But, for now, let's continue to style.

Style

The Associated Press Stylebook

The style guide used within the field of communications, and therefore within public relations, is The Associated Press Stylebook and Briefing on Media Law. "Updated regularly since its initial publication in 1953, the AP Stylebook is a must-have reference for writers, editors, students and professionals. It provides fundamental guidelines for spelling, language, punctuation, usage and journalistic style" (What is the AP Stylebook?, n.d.).

More commonly referred to as "AP Style," the AP Stylebook serves as the "definitive resource for writers" and as "the bible for journalists and anyone who cares about good writing" (The Associated Press Stylebook, 2017, foreword). Because PR writing takes its cues from journalistic writing, the AP Stylebook can also be considered the bible for PR practitioners.

Available in both print and digital formats, the AP Stylebook is "widely used as a writing and editing reference in newsrooms, classrooms and corporate offices worldwide" (Maks, 2019, para. 5). The classic print edition is published each spring and the online edition is updated throughout the year by a team of editors who are committed to the goal of producing writing that its "clear, fair and concise" (The Associated Press Stylebook, 2017, foreword).

At more than 600 pages and organized alphabetically like a dictionary, the AP Stylebook can be daunting, even for the most experienced communications professionals. Furthermore, it is updated regularly with new entries and, sometimes, changes to existing entries. In addition to its entries, it also has sections devoted to specific topics. The 2019 edition, for example, has special sections examining punctuation, business, data journalism, polls and surveys, health and science, social media guidelines, religion, sports, food, fashion, media law, broadcast and more.

AP Style also provides guidance for writing about all types of diversity. Whether it be age, race, ethnicity, gender, sexuality, disability, mental illness, substance abuse, marital status, diseases, religion or name usage (e.g., Arabic names, Chinese names, Spanish names, etc.), AP Style has an entry for it. The 2019 edition, for example, includes a new entry called *race-related coverage*, which provides guidance for writing about issues involving race.

To help ease the process of learning the language of AP Style, I've introduced some of the most important "must-knows" from the AP Stylebook below. These select AP Style entries are, in my experience, the most-used in public relations writing. They are also, in my opinion, the most fundamental to AP Style.

Once you've mastered these basic entries, I encourage you to explore additional terms, especially those that most apply to the industry your organization falls within. For example, helpful entries for PR practitioners working in academia would be "academic degrees," "academic departments," "academic titles," "adviser," "alumnus, alumni, alumna, alumnae," "doctor," "professor" and more.

Learning the book's intricacies will never, and should never, stop, especially with new editions and revisions each year. In fact, it should be a daily occurrence. I suggest you bring it to class, bring it to work, keep it on your desk (or on your phone or iPad!) and always nearby. Live it, love it and learn its language that will give you the structure to approach all types of communications writing with consistency and confidence. Think of the AP Stylebook as your new best friend. It's the beginning of a beautiful, lifelong relationship.

AP Style "Must-Knows"

- abbreviations and acronyms
- academic degrees
- academic titles
- accent marks
- accused
- addiction
- addresses
- ages
- alcoholic
- allege
- ampersand (&)
- a.m., p.m.
- animals
- annual
- Arabic names
- arrest
- attribution
- boy, girl
- brand names
- bylines

- capitalization
- chairman, chairwoman
- Chinese names
- cities and towns
- citizen, resident, subject, national, native
- cliches, jargon
- company, companies
- company names
- composition titles
- compound adjectives
- corporation
- council, councilor, councilman, councilwoman
- courtesy titles
- datelines
- dates
- days of the week
- decades
- dialect
- dictionaries
- dimensions
- directions and regions
- disabled, handicapped
- diseases
- distances
- divorce
- doctor
- dwarf
- e.g.
- elderly
- events
- family names
- female
- first lady, first gentleman
- foreign names
- fractions
- gay
- gender
- geographic names
- gods and goddesses
- headlines
- his, her
- holidays and holy days
- hometown
- husband, wife
- i.e.
- immigration

- indict
- initials
- injuries
- initials
- italics
- junior, senior
- Korean names
- lady
- last
- late
- legislative titles
- LGBT/LGBTQ
- magazine names
- mailman
- mental illness
- mentally disabled, intellectually disabled, developmentally disabled
- middle initials
- middle names
- midget
- midnight
- military titles
- months
- more than, over
- names
- newspaper names
- noon
- numerals
- on
- percent, percentage, percentage points
- Portuguese names
- possessives
- prison, jail
- privacy
- pseudonyms, nicknames
- quotations in the news
- race-related coverage
- ranges
- reference works
- religious references
- religious titles
- Roman numerals
- Russian names
- same-sex marriage
- seasons
- second reference
- sentences

- Spanish names
- speeches
- spokesman, spokeswoman, spokesperson
- state
- state names
- sue
- survivor, victim
- suspect
- telephone numbers
- temperatures
- time element
- titles
- today, tonight
- tomorrow
- toward
- trademark
- upward
- URL
- web
- website
- weights
- woman, women
- years
- yesterday
- youth
- ZIP code

❖ PERSPECTIVE FROM THE PROS

By Heidi Carr

Quick! What's the plural for "syllabus"? If you said "syllabi," you were... WRONG!

Don't believe me? It's right there on Page 275.

How about calculating your body mass index? (Page 36 will tell you how).

Can you find out what passengers on a nightmare cruise are posting on social media? (Page 368–372).

As you go through your career, you'll be amazed at all the fabulous tidbits of information tucked away in the pages of The Associated Press Stylebook.

It also is a reflection of our society through the decades. For example, the 2019 AP Stylebook contains lengthy entries on alt-right, fake news and terrorism. These items weren't even mentioned a few years ago.

Some entries that once merited a small mention, such as illegal immigration and gender, now have a full page dedicated to them.

And some entries have evolved or completely disappeared. There have been times when the stylebook dictated usage of the words negro, colored and black. You won't find any of those entries in today's stylebook, although you will find them among the 6 1/2 pages dedicated to Race-Related Coverage.

As you flip through your book, you'll come across some gems. Here are a few that have made me chuckle over the years.

1. **The "f" in French dressing is capitalized, but in french fries, it's lowercased.**
   French refers to the style of cut of the potatoes, not the country. (Page 451)

2. **Journalism is referred to as the "Fourth Estate."**
   Historically, English society was divided into three estates: the Lords Spiritual (the clergy), the Lords Temporal (the nobility) and the Commons (the bourgeoisie). According to the stylebook (Page 116), Edmund Burke referred to the reporters' gallery in Parliament as the "Fourth Estate."

3. **Why is it called *marijuana*?**
   Outside of the United States, you're more likely to hear the word cannabis than marijuana. That's because the term marijuana started being used in the United States in the early twentieth century by those wanting to boost anti-Mexican sentiment. (Pages 176–177)

4. **What is Santa Claus' real name?**
   Kriss Kringle (note there are two s's.) The name comes from *Christkindl.* You can also call him Santa or Santa Claus on first reference. But on second reference, Santa is nice; Claus is naughty. (Page 162 and 256)

5. **Toward, afterward, backward, forward**
   There's no 's' at the end of any of these. The AP Stylebook doesn't explain why, but a lot of grammarians have weighed in, explaining that in Great Britain, the words towards, afterwards, backwards and forwards are used, but nineteenth-century Americans deemed these spellings too pretentious. (Pages 288, 8, 28 and 115)

6. **Don't gibe me.**
   To gibe means to taunt; to jibe means to shift direction or agree. (Page 124) I have to look it up every time.

7. **Alright is _not_ all right.**
   There's no such word as alright. (Page 13) Got it? All right!

8. **Give me a "P"! (But don't give me a hyphen.)**
   It's "pompom." No space between the poms. (Page 471)

9. **It's Daylight Saving Time (not Savings)**

The time change takes effect at 2 a.m. on the second Sunday of March until 2 a.m. on the first Sunday of November. (Page 80) Remember: fall back, spring forward.

10. **Oh, no! The flying disc flew into the hot tub. Hand me a tissue.**

Frisbee is a trademarked name, meaning unless you know for sure it's a Frisbee, you have to call it a flying disc. Same goes for Kleenex (tissue), Bubble Wrap (packaging material), Jacuzzi (hot tub), Band-Aid (bandage), Kitty Litter (cat litter), Q-tips (cotton swabs), Popsicle (ice pop), Ziplock (zip-close bag), AstroTurf (artificial grass) and my least favorite: Jet Ski (personal watercraft). There are dozens of 'em that have seeped into our daily vocabulary.

11. **Don't call her Mrs. West.**

It's Kim Kardashian West on first reference, Kardashian West on second reference. (Page 160) She joins Hillary Rodham Clinton, Adolf Hitler and Manolo Blahnik as being among the very few whose names have an AP Style. (Pages 53, 138 and 464)

12. **New Year's Six**

There are six college football games that rotate the College Football Playoff semifinal games typically played on New Year's Eve or New Year's Day. The games are: the Orange Bowl, the Fiesta Bowl, the Peach Bowl, the Cotton Bowl, the Rose Bowl and the Sugar Bowl. (Page 432) As a college student, you may want to know that.

13. **"First annual" is just wishful thinking.**

There's no such thing as a "first annual" anything — it has to have happened at least once for it to become an annual event. (Page 18)

14. **There are really only 538 votes that matter.**

There have been five times in U.S. history when the Electoral College resulted in the candidate winning the presidency despite losing the popular vote. (Page 97)

15. **Pitbull v. Pit Bull**

A pit bull is a dog. Pitbull is Mr. 305. (OK, that's not in the Stylebook. But it should be)

16. **Twenty-six places to see in your lifetime**

There are seven continents (Page 67); five oceans (Page 208); Seven Seas (Page 260) and Seven Wonders of the World. (page 260)

17. **April Fools!**

The apostrophe goes after the "s" in April Fools' Day. Apparently there's more than one fool. (Page 21)

18. **Ice Age**

There have been several ice ages in the earth's history. The most recent started 1.6 million years ago and just ended 10,000 years ago. Talk about a drop in the proverbial bucket. (Page 142)

19. **What does the "S" in Harry S. Truman stand for?**

Nothing! He only had a middle initial, not a middle name. Truman once said he didn't care whether the "S" was followed by a period. AP cares, and says use the period. (Page 290)

20. **That's baloney!**

Bologna is what you put in a sandwich; baloney is foolish talk.

So when professors say they are handing out their "syllabi," you can politely tell them after class that the plural of syllabus is really syllabuses. Remember, nobody likes a smart aleck. (Look it up)

Grammar/Usage

AP Style also provides helpful guidance on grammar style and usage. Below, I've included a basic list of entries related to grammar and word usage:

- a, an
- accept, except
- adverse, averse
- affect, effect
- afterward
- amid
- among, between
- amount, number
- ampersand (&)
- backward
- bad, badly
- because, since
- beside, besides
- collective nouns
- complement, compliment
- compose, comprise, constitute
- contractions
- couple of
- damage, damages
- dangling modifiers
- dyeing, dying
- each
- each other, one another
- either
- either … or, neither … nor
- em dash, en dash, hyphen
- ensure, insure, assure
- entitled

- essential clauses, nonessential clauses
- essential phrases, nonessential phrases
- every one, everyone
- different
- farther, further
- fewer, less
- flier, flyer
- forward
- good, well
- hang, hanged, hung
- historic, historical
- in, into
- include
- irregardless
- like, as
- it's, its
- last
- late
- lay, lie
- -ly
- off, of
- plurals
- possessives
- should, would
- spelling
- than, then
- that (conjunction)
- that, which (pronouns)
- their, there, they're
- that, them, their
- verbs
- who's, whose
- who, whom

Punctuation

Proper punctuation is so important that AP Style dedicates an entire section to it. "Incorrect punctuation can change the meaning of a sentence, the results of which could be far-reaching. Even if the meaning is not changed, bad punctuation, however inconsequential, can cause the reader to lose track of what is being said and give up reading a sentence" (The Associated Press, 2019, p. 320).

Although you should read this section in its entirety (and more than once, because it's a lot to digest), I've listed the punctuation entries that you'll use most in public relations writing:

- apostrophe (')
- colon (:)
- comma (,)
- dash (—)
- exclamation point (!)
- hyphen (-)
- periods (.)
- quotation marks (" ")

Editing Marks

AP Style also provides writers with a system of symbols for editing. Editing marks include symbols to indicate edits such as "indent for paragraph," "spell it out," "abbreviate," "uppercase," "lowercase," "remove space," "insert space," "delete," "insert comma," "insert apostrophe," and "insert period," among others.

Flip to the table of contents of your AP Stylebook to find the section called "Editing marks." If you have the 2019 edition, this section appears on Page 540. Review the full page of editing marks; you'll soon be putting them into practice with the end-of-chapter exercises.

Beyond the chapter exercises, begin using these editing marks when revising and/or proofing public relations writing of all types in all contexts. For example, as a public relations manager, I used AP Style's editing marks when reviewing PR writing produced by public relations coordinators. I also used them when reviewing my own work or when asking public relations managers or directors to edit my writing. Today, as a communications faculty member who teaches PR writing, I continue to use AP Style's editing marks when providing feedback to students or when asking them to edit each other's work.

Form

Inverted Pyramid

Similar to style, public relations writing takes its cues from journalism when it comes to form. With the exception of feature writing (Chapter 12), which has its own form, this form takes its shape through the inverted pyramid — a method of reporting news and organizing our writing. Sterin and Winston (2018) define the inverted pyramid as a "reporting structure wherein the most important facts are presented in the lead sentences, followed by more elaborate details that support those facts" (p. 472).

The inverted pyramid is represented by an upside pyramid, or triangle, and organizes information from most important to least important. The very top of the pyramid is represented by the most newsworthy information — the who, what, where, when, why and, if applicable, the how. This information is communicated in the opening sentence or paragraph and is referred to as the "lede" or "nut graph."

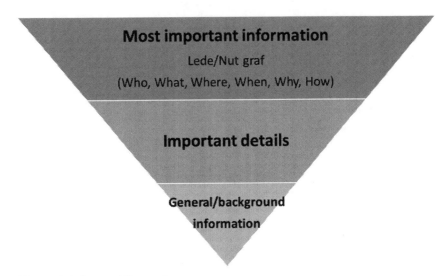

Figure 1.1 Inverted Pyramid.

"In journalism, the *lede* refers to the introductory section of a news story that is intended to entice the reader to read the full story," (Why do We 'Bury the Lede?', 2019, para. 1).

Whereas feature writing may delay the lede in order to entice the reader (also called a "soft lede"), news writing gets straight to the point.

When crafting a news release about an upcoming health fair, for example, the lede might read:

Global Health Co. invites members of the community to take part in free health screenings and seminars at its annual health fair taking place Tuesday, April 7, 2020, from 10 a.m. to 2 p.m. at Klyde Warren Park in Dallas. Now in its fifth year, the fair is expected to host more than 1,500 attendees in support of World Health Day.

In two sentences, the "lede" communicates the "who," (Global Health Co.), the "what" (annual health fair), the "where" (Klyde Warren Park), the "when," (Tuesday, April 7) and the "why," (to support World Health Day).

Once the writer communicates the most newsworthy information to readers through the "lede," he or she should next state important details. These details might include:

During the event, attendees will have the opportunity to take part in screenings for blood pressure, cholesterol, body mass index (BMI), bone density, hearing and others. They can also check out various seminars related to health, wellness and lifestyle.

In addition to offering health screenings and seminars, the fair will feature healthy cooking demonstrations, yoga sessions and a variety of wellness-related vendors.

"Global Health Co. is proud to partner with local health and wellness professionals to host its fifth annual health fair in support of World Health Day," said Amanda Lennox, CEO of Global Health Co. "We hope the Dallas community will join us for a fun-filled day dedicated to health."

Important details are then followed by general information, represented by the bottom portion of the pyramid. General information is considered the least newsworthy but is still relevant to the reader. An example of general information for the health fair could be:

The Global Health Co. health fair was started in 2015 as a way to bring awareness to World Health Day while furthering the company's mission to democratize health locally and globally.

Attendees can view the full schedule of events and register for free screenings by visiting www.globalhealthcorp.com/healthfair

For more information about Global Health Co., visit www.globalhealthcorp.com/about

Whether you're writing a memo, a news release, a bio sketch, a pitch or any other type of PR writing, you can use the inverted pyramid to structure and summarize your writing, so that you don't "bury the lede" and keep readers guessing.

"The conventions of the inverted pyramid require the reporter to summarize the story, to get to the heart, to the point, to sum up quickly and concisely the answer to the question: What's the news? The pyramid approach addresses the most important questions at the top of the story. It states the thesis and then provides supporting material" (Scanlan, 2003, para. 6).

Rules Related to Structure

In addition to organizing content using the inverted pyramid, rules related to the form/structure of journalistic and public relations writing include:

- Use short sentences and short paragraphs and get your point across with as few words as possible; don't overwrite or overstate.
- Use block paragraphs (left aligned, no indentation, with a line space between paragraphs).
- Use one space between sentences (see "sentences" entry in AP Stylebook).
- Allow quotes to stand alone in their own paragraphs.
- Write headlines in present tense when possible (e.g., "Global Health Co. *hosts its fifth annual health fair*").
- Use headlines that capitalize only the first word and proper nouns (also known as Downstyle; see "headlines" entry in AP Stylebook).
- When attributing sources, use "said" for news writing and "says" for feature/magazine writing.

While inverted pyramid and the above bullets are central to the art of public relations writing, it's important to note that certain types of PR writing will also feature elements unique to their form. For example, news releases, include a dateline, a boilerplate and a ### or -30-, among other elements. But more on that in Chapter 2.

❖ PERSPECTIVE FROM THE PROS

By Megan Fitzgerald

From the time we first begin weaving stories together in elementary school, we are taught that stories start at the beginning, move to the middle, and wrap up at the end. While chronological order has its place, news writing isn't it. News follows the inverted pyramid style — most important first then work your way down to the least important. We start with the who, what, where, when, why and how. Then, we go from there.

My husband, who is in the Coast Guard, learned the importance of this when he came home a week before our third child was due and launched into a very lengthy story about how his commanding officer had called and that my husband's name was on a list of service members being called to deploy out of the country for nearly a year. As my chest tightened and panic waved over me, he, finally, got to the end of the story. He had been passed over for this deployment because of the impending birth of our child.

In our house, this story would be considered breaking news. This is not the time to start stories at the beginning, drag your audience through the middle, and eventually get to the end. Inverted pyramid style tosses conventional story telling aside and gets right to the point. As I explained to my husband, he needed to start with the most important information — that he's not actually deploying — and then give me the details, saving a very pregnant wife from unnecessary stress.

Inverted pyramid style gives the audience what they need to know first and then works through the details and supporting information. Although it's up to the audience to decide how far into a story they want to go, using the inverted pyramid style guarantees the writer that he or she has given the audience what they need to know.

Tone

It's important that we, as public relations practitioners, remember that public relations writing has an organizational purpose, and that we are writing with specific publics in mind. Our writing should not be deeply personal, nor should it express our thoughts and feelings.

As a public relations writer, you are not aiming to create works of art. Don't make the mistake of thinking that good public relations writing is like a song, or like poetry or prose, full of descriptive phrasing and obscure thoughts. There are times when creative writing is necessary, but creativity should never overshadow what's most important about a public relations message: its ability to communicate information in a way that people will understand.

(Zappala & Carden, 2010, p. 4)

Most public relations writing uses a third-person point of view and avoids personal pronouns, such as "I," "we" and "you," although there are instances where a "you-focused" and conversational tone might be appropriate, such as writing for an employee newsletter, crafting a media pitch targeting a specific journalist, or when communicating with an organization's followers on social media.

While PR writers are certainly not novelists or song writers, there are specific instances where public relations practitioners have the ability to be more creative in their writing while still remaining clear, objective and honest. A few examples where creative writing may be appropriate in public relations include:

- Feature Writing (e.g., "Get the Scoop on the Best Summer Ice Cream Flavors")
- When assisting advertising/marketing departments with copy
- Op-ed Articles, which are clearly labeled as opinion pieces

In Chapter 12, we'll examine feature writing more closely, including examples of creative, or anecdotal, ledes.

Honest, Objective, Clear and Concise

Public relations writing takes many forms, which are explored throughout this text. Whether we're engaging in news writing, feature writing or any other type of PR writing, the tone of PR writing should always remain the same; it should be *honest, objective, clear* and *concise*.

Like journalists, PR writers are charged with being *honest* and *objective*. We do not insert our opinion into our writing, nor do we twist the facts to make the client look good. We report only the truth, and we aim to avoid bias even in the most subtle of ways. For example, when attributing sources, we simply say "said" or "says." We do not use loaded verbs such as "exclaimed," "gasped," "shrieked," etc., which could imply bias.

We also do not use vague modifiers that could imply bias. Rather than using ambiguous words like "very" or "slightly," we should be as specific as possible. For example, instead of stating a fundraiser was "very successful," the writer could be clearer and more precise by saying "the event raised over $100,000 for cancer research."

Although we, as writers, do not insert our opinion when crafting public relations materials, there are instances when it is appropriate, and necessary, to include the thoughts and opinions of others. By quoting sources or paraphrasing their words, we can attribute thoughts and opinions to a specific person while remaining objective as the writer.

Let's revisit the Global Health Co. health fair example to illustrate how this might work. While it would be biased for the writer to state "Members of the community are invited to attend the most anticipated and exciting event of the year," the writer *can* include similar sentiments if he or she attributes them to a specific source. For example:

> *"We invite members of the community to take charge of their health at this exciting and life-changing event," said Amanda Lennox, CEO of Global Health Co.*

In addition to communicating honestly and objectively, we also need to communicate *clearly* in a way that won't confuse the reader. Rather than using technical jargon, select a simpler version of the word. For example, instead of using the word "utilize," say "use." Instead of saying "viable," say "practical." Instead of saying "optimum," say "best."

The "cliches, jargon" entry in the AP Stylebook also offers guidance on crafting clear language. "Cliches are the junk food of the literary pantry, much loved by lazy writers ... Don't push readers away, or lull them to sleep. Engage them with original, specific phrasing" (The Associated Press, 2019, p. 52).

Beyond using simple language, PR writers should also strive to use simple sentences. If a sentence seems too long and complicated, break it down into two sentences.

> Most newspapers are written at about a ninth-grade reading level so everybody with that level of education or more—the majority of readers—should be able to understand the articles, columns, and editorials ... If you are preparing a news release or guest editorial for such a publication, plan on writing for readers with a ninth-grade reading ability.
>
> (Smith, 2017, p. 233)

Finally, public relations writing is *concise* and is characterized by short sentences and short paragraphs. By using the inverted pyramid, we can structure our writing in a way that allows us to communicate the most important details quickly before we lose the reader's attention. Edit mercilessly to omit needless words, phrases and sentences. Get to the point before you "bury the lede."

Exercises

Exercise 1.1 – AP Style Editing Symbols

Locate the section in your Associated Press Stylebook called "Editing Marks" and read it. Next, correct the below using the proper editing marks.

a.	Uppercase	The company is located in Rochester, New york.
b.	Lowercase	The Weather is adverse.
c.	Insert Space	Joe Biden is running for president of the UnitedStates.

d.	Insert Word	Anne Smith, Ph.D., presented at conference.
e.	Delete	Hawaii Hawaii is not abbreviated in datelines or stories.
f.	Transpose	The Awards Academy are presented annually.
g.	Insert Comma(s)	Monday Feb. 3 2020
h.	Insert Period	An altar is a table-like platform
i.	Insert Quotation	We are deeply saddened by the news," the spokeswoman said.
j.	Abbreviate	BIRMINGHAM, Alabama

Exercise 1.2 – Inverted Pyramid Style

Chapter 1 introduced the inverted pyramid as the form used by journalists and public relations professionals to structure their writing. Using inverted pyramid style, reorder the paragraphs below.

Learn more about Farmhouse Foods' Holy Cow! line by visiting www.farmhousefoods.com/holycow or following it on Facebook, Twitter and Instagram @holycowmilks

Holy Cow! milks will be available for purchase by the half gallon and as 8-ounce single servings that come in a case of eight. An 8-ounce serving is 150 calories, contains 8 grams of protein and accounts for 20% of the recommended daily value for calcium.

All Holy Cow! milks are free of artificial flavors and colors and contain DHA Omega-3 to support brain and eye health. Other ingredients include: Grade A Low-fat Organic Milk, Organic Cane Sugar, Organic Natural Flavor, Salt, Vitamin A and Vitamin D3.

On Wednesday, April 1, Farmhouse Foods Inc. will launch an organic line of flavored milks called Holy Cow! that will be sold in more than 10,000 stores nationwide. The line is USDA certified organic and features low-fat milk in three flavors: chocolate, strawberry and vanilla.

Exercise 1.3 – Defining Public Relations

Chapter 1 explored various definitions of public relations offered by academics, authors and industry organizations. Locate a definition of public relations that was not covered in Chapter 1 and include the author/source. Compare and contrast this definition and the others explored in Chapter 1. What are the similarities and differences?

References

About. (2008). Retrieved from www.cprs.ca/About.aspx
About, P.R. (n.d.). Retrieved from www.cipr.co.uk/content/about-us/about-pr
Bethell, R. (n.d.). Public Relations. Retrieved from www.mepra.org/about-us/
    public-relations/

Broom, G.M., & Sha, B. (2013). *Cutlip & Center's Effective Public Relations* (11th ed.). United States of America: Pearson Education, Inc.

Maks, P. (2019, May 29). Health and science chapter debuts in 2019 AP Stylebook. Retrieved from www.ap.org/press-releases/2019/health-and-science-chapter-debuts-in-2019-ap-stylebook

Learn About PR. (2019). Retrieved from http://prssa.prsa.org/about-prssa/learn-about-pr/

Scanlan, C. (2003, June 20). Writing from the Top Down: Pros and Cons of the Inverted Pyramid. Retrieved from www.poynter.org/reporting-editing/2003/writing-from-the-top-down-pros-and-cons-of-the-inverted-pyramid/

Smith, R.D. (2017). *Strategic Planning for Public Relations* (5th ed.). New York, NY: Routledge.

Stacks, D.W. (2017). *Primer of Public Relations Research* (3rd ed.). New York, NY: The Guilford Press.

Sterin, C.S., & Winston, T. (2018). *Mass Media Revolution* (3rd ed.). New York, NY: Routledge.

The Associated Press (2017). *The Associated Press Stylebook 2017 and Briefing on Media Law.* New York, NY: The Associated Press.

The Associated Press (2019). *The Associated Press Stylebook 2019 and Briefing on Media Law.* New York, NY: The Associated Press.

Universal Accreditation Board (2015). *Study Guide for the Certificate in Principles of Public Relations Examination* (2nd ed.).

Universal Accreditation Board (2017). *Study Guide for the Examination for Accreditation in Public Relations.* (4th ed.).

What is the AP Stylebook? (n.d.). Retrieved from www.apstylebook.com/help?query=USAGE#/questions/210938-What-is-the-AP-Stylebook

What is it? (2019). Retrieved from www.pria.com.au/public-relations/what-is-it/

Why Do We 'Bury the Lede?' (2019, July 1). Retrieved from www.merriam-webster.com/words-at-play/bury-the-lede-versus-lead

Wilcox, D.L., Cameron, G.T., & Reber, B.H. (2016). *Public Relations: Strategies and Tactics* (11th ed.). United States of America: Pearson Education, Inc.

Zappala, J.M., & Carden, A.R. (2010). *Public Relations Writing Worktext: A Practical Guide for the Profession* (3rd ed.). New York, NY: Routledge.

Media Relations

Chapter 2

News Releases and Other Types of Releases

Whitney Lehmann and Michael Laderman

In Chapter 1, we discussed how public relations practitioners manage the flow of information between an organization and its various publics. This next section of the text introduces forms of public relations writing that practitioners use when communicating with the media, including news releases, media pitches, media advisories/alerts, public service announcements and media kits.

Just as I feel that those who communicate well can do just about anything, I also believe that those who can master the news release can write all other public relations materials, which is why I have chosen to kick off this journey of PR writing with how to write a traditional news release.

Purpose

News releases, also referred to as *press releases*, are used by public relations practitioners for several reasons:

- To communicate a one-time event (e.g., product launch or employee promotion).
- To communicate a re-occurring event (e.g., annual holiday drive or highlights from a company's annual report).
- To communicate an upcoming event (also known as an "advance").
- To communicate an event that has already happened (also known as a "post release").
- To communicate updates on an ongoing matter (e.g., a company recall or other crisis that may require multiple updates).
- To distribute multimedia elements to the media or other publics (such as a photo release, video news release or social media release).
- And more!

Structure

In Chapter 1, we reviewed the must-know style guidelines for public relations writing: Associated Press Style, inverted pyramid, correct grammar and punctuation, block paragraphs, proper use of quotations and attribution, sensitivity to diversity, and so on.

We also reviewed tone, and how most public relations writing is written from the third-person point of view and uses pronouns such as he, him, his, himself, she, her, hers, herself, it, its, itself, they, them, their, theirs and themselves. News releases fall into the third-person category and are written with a factual tone.

In addition to these general style rules, it's important to know that each piece of public relations writing follows a certain structure and contains certain components — an anatomy, per se. For each piece of PR writing covered in this worktext, I have outlined its structure and included a template that will help you to learn its "anatomy."

Although each piece of PR writing does have a set structure and flow with certain components, it's also important to know that each company or organization will also incorporate its own style guidelines and branding, including fonts, type sizes, logos, colors, etc. While the templates will give you structure, your organizations will give you style.

Let's jump in by beginning with the structure of a news release:

- **Logo:** The first element of a news release is the organization's logo. Make sure to use the logo specified by the client's brand guidelines and be careful not to distort or stretch the logo. Depending on the client's style for news releases, the logo can be aligned left, centered or aligned right. The template provided below aligns the logo to the left.

  Note: At times, news releases may include more than one logo. For example, when a client partners with another organization on an event or initiative, include both organizations' logos.

- **FOR IMMEDIATE RELEASE:** Often written in all capital letters, "FOR IMMEDIATE RELEASE" is accompanied by the release date — the date that the release information can be publicly distributed. This includes the month (abbreviated in AP Style if applicable), day and year. For example, "Feb. 6, 2017" or "June 30, 2017." Sometimes a release may be *embargoed* until a certain date, meaning that the information it contains cannot be publicly distributed until that specified date.
- **Media Contact:** The communications or PR person issuing the release on behalf of a company or organization should include his or her name, phone number and email, so that members of the media or public can contact this person with any questions.
- **Headline:** The headline of a release should summarize what the news release is about in as few words as possible with verbs traditionally written in present tense (see exception below). For example, "Sunshine State University Healthy Heart event raises $200,000 for American Heart Association" or "Sunshine State University names Elizabeth Bailey as provost."

  Some more tips for headline writing:
  - AP Style calls for headlines to be written in "**Down style**," meaning that only the first word of the headline and proper nouns are capitalized. For example, "More than 700 people attend annual health and wellness event

at Klyde Warren Park." "**Up Style**," on the other hand, capitalizes all words with four or more letters. For example, "More Than 700 People Attend Annual Health and Wellness Event at Hyde Park."

Note: The New York Times and People magazine are two well-known publications that break this AP Style rule and use Up Style.

○ Headlines typically **do not use articles** such a, an, the. They are simply omitted. For example:

"Sunshine State University hosts heart-healthy event" versus "Sunshine State University hosts a heart-healthy event"

○ Headlines **do not** end with a period.
○ AP Style calls for **single quotes within headlines**. For example: "Sunshine State University presents 'MLK: A Dream' art exhibit during Black History Month"
○ AP Style calls for **numerals within headlines**. For example: "Student-produced film wins 7 awards at Fort Lauderdale Film Festival"
○ Headlines are typically formatted in **bold** with a **larger type size** than the rest of the news release. A common type size for headlines is 24.
○ While **headlines aim to use verbs in present tense**, an exception to this rule would be when using a verb in present tense results in your organization becoming the object of the headline rather than the subject of the headline. In this case, the writer may use a verb in past tense in order to **keep the organization the focus of the headline**. For example, "Sunshine State University professor awarded $1 million grant from U.S. Department of State" versus "U.S. Department of State awards Sunshine State University professor $1 million grant"

● **Subhead:** A subhead can be used to include additional information with a headline when needed. For the headline "Sunshine State University Healthy Heart event raises $200,000 for American Heart Association," an appropriate headline might be, "Student-run event features live music, yoga, meditation and more on Fort Lauderdale Beach."

○ Subheads follow the **same rules mentioned above for headlines**.

Some exceptions, however:
○ Although subheads are typically formatted with a **larger type size** than the rest of the news release, they use a **type size smaller than the headline**. A common type size for subheads is 16 or 18.
○ Subheads are typically **not bolded** but are typically formatted with **italics**.

Sunshine State University Healthy Heart event raises $200,000 for American Heart Association
Student-run event features live music, yoga, meditation and more on Fort Lauderdale Beach

● **Dateline:** The dateline states the city (and state if applicable) where the news originates from. The city is written in all capital letters. The state, if included, is not in all CAPS and is abbreviated, if necessary, per AP Style (Alaska, Hawaii,

Idaho, Iowa, Maine, Ohio, Texas and Utah are never abbreviated). For example, "FORT LAUDERDALE, Fla." AP Style calls for certain well-known U.S. and international cities, such as Miami, Boston, Chicago, Milan, Madrid, London and others to stand alone. "For example, "MIAMI." All others not specified by AP Style are followed by their respective state.

- **Body of Release:** The copy of a news release should follow **inverted pyramid style** (Chapter 1) and use **block paragraphs** (no indentation) that are aligned left with single spacing between sentences and a line space between paragraphs. The copy should use a smaller type than the headline/subhead. Common type sizes for the body of the release are 11 point or 12 point.

Other elements within the body of a news release:

- ○ **Lede/Nut graph:** The "lede" or "nut graph" of your release is the first one to two sentences or paragraphs and communicates the who, what, where, when, why and how of your release.
- ○ **Quotes:** Quotes should stand alone as their own paragraphs and should support, and speak to, the paragraph directly before them. Make sure to include a well-rounded variety of voices. For example, in the template below, students and the university president are quoted. Other options would have been to include quotes from attendees at the event or from a representative of the American Heart Association.

Other tips for using quotes:

- As covered in Chapter 1, the proper attribution for quotes uses "said." For example, "John Smith, said" or "said John Smith, vice president of finance." Attribution should be set off using a comma. For example, "The exhibit is a cultural showcase," said Morgan Manley, a sophomore at Sunshine State University. For quotes longer than one sentence, attribution should be used at the end of the first sentence to introduce the speaker as early as possible.
- Any quotes within quotes use single quotes. For example, "During Black History Month, we examine Martin Luther King Jr.'s 'I Have a Dream' speech," said Jayne Woods, assistant professor of history for Sunshine State University.
- If the person's title comes before their name, AP Style calls for the title to be capitalized. For example, "Sunshine State University President Charleston Stanton" versus "Charleston Stanton, president of Sunshine State University."
- ○ **-more-:** For news releases longer than one page, this indicates that release copy continues on the next page. Place -more- at the bottom of the page to indicate to the reader that the news release continues on the next page.
- ○ **For More Information:** The final paragraph of a news release typically directs readers to where they can find more information. This could be a phone number, an email address, a URL, an organization's social media channels, etc. For example, "For more information on Sunshine State University's Winter Holiday Drive and how to donate, call 555-555-5555, email winterdrive@SSU.edu or visit www.ssu.edu/winterdrive

- **Boilerplate:** A boilerplate is a concise paragraph that summarizes the mission, key facts, and, often, history of a company or organization. Think of it as a client's "About Us" statement. Boilerplates should be updated regularly and as needed, especially as facts change. For example, a boilerplate that includes the line "Sunshine State University is home to 10,000 undergraduate and 5,000 graduate students" would need to be updated as those numbers change.

  Note: At times, news releases contain more than one boilerplate, for example, an organization's main boilerplate along with a boilerplate for one of its specific entities, events or initiatives. Another instance would be including the boilerplate for a partnering organization or sponsor. In that case, make sure to list your organization's boilerplate first.

- **### or -30-:** The ### or -30- indicates the end of a release. Whether a company uses the ## or -30- is a style preference. A company may also create their own version of ### or -30- for branding purposes. For example, Seminole Hard Rock Hotel & Casino Hollywood uses -SHR- to indicate the end of its releases. When looking at different examples of news releases, you will notice that the ### or -30- can come before or after the boilerplate. The template included with this worktext uses a ### after the boilerplate.

❖ PERSPECTIVE FROM THE PROS

By Jeremy Katzman

I started my first job in public relations well after the days of mailing printed press releases with photos and captions taped to the paper. But the evolution of the field from 2005 to now might as well be like comparing hieroglyphics on a cave wall to the invention of the printing press. Facebook was just getting started and Tom was everyone's friend on MySpace. YouTube and Twitter were not yet household names. Instagram and SnapChat weren't even a figment of Silicon Valley's imagination. Traditional media was widely respected, unquestioned and was the primary source of news for most of us. Things have changed, and they continue to transform rapidly.

While the media continue to evolve, people's thirst for information and news is thriving. The difference is, more content than ever is easily available, facts are in question and attention spans are at an all-time low.

The purpose of a news release is to provide timely, useful and accurate information to the audience. The primary readers used to be reporters, but increasingly, companies have the ability to speak directly to the end user — the customer.

News releases must be clear, concise and interesting to garner attention. What previously would have been used as a reference for reporters is now commonly repurposed or linked to verbatim.

The lesson is write for your end user, not the reporter and not for your client. Tell a story. Make it relevant to them. And don't be too self-serving or you will lose brand loyalty and trust.

I have lectured many times on "Making Research Sound Sexy to Secure Results." You may ask, "how could research possibly sound sexy?" As communicators, we must be detectives — find the useful information, highlight it and tell people why it should matter to them.

Take this research headline for example. "Regulation and dysregulation of mammalian nucleotide excision repair: a pathway to non-germline breast carcinogenesis."

This may catch the attention of a few Ph.D.s, but most people would scroll right past this. After interviewing the scientist and asking the same question five different ways to finally understand the purpose of this work and the implications of the findings, I rewrote the headline, "Researchers discover DNA repair is high in heart, nonexistent in brain — results could help explain causes of dementia and memory loss."

This new headline garnered significant impressions compared to other research results, and the scientists were pleased. I encourage you to follow some of these tips and ultimately be an advocate not only for your client or company, but for your audience. Your news releases will be a valuable tool in your success.

News Release Template

Now that we've reviewed all of the elements that comprise a news release, let's bring them all together by looking at the news release template below. Notes highlighted/in italics indicate places on the release where one should be careful to incorporate AP Style rules; these notes should be deleted. I've also included style and structure tips.

LOGO
FOR IMMEDIATE RELEASE
Feb. 6, 2017 *[All dates should be written in AP Style.]*

Media Contact:
John Smith
555-555-5555 *[All phone numbers should be written in AP Style.]*
johnsmith@email.com

Headline should use Down style, present tense and a large type size such as 24 point

If a subhead is needed, type it directly underneath in italics in a smaller type size such as 16 point

FORT LAUDERDALE, Fla. — On Monday, Feb. 6, Sunshine State University (SSU) students gathered on Fort Lauderdale Beach to host Healthy Hearts, the university's annual fundraiser benefitting the American Heart Association as part of American Heart Month in February. More than 700 people from the tri-county area attended the event. *[The city and state (if applicable) forming the dateline of a release should be written in AP Style.]*

The day-long event, which ran from 10 a.m. to 8 p.m., featured live music, beach yoga, cardio and strength-training exercises, meditation courses, cooking demonstrations and other heart-healthy activities. Day passes for the event cost $25 with all proceeds benefiting the Greater Fort Lauderdale affiliate of the American Heart Association. *[News releases use block paragraphs with no indentation. Paragraphs should be brief with no more than 2–3 sentences. Use single spacing between sentences and double spacing between paragraphs.]*

"I have heart disease in my family, so I'm proud and passionate to be part of an event dedicated to fighting the disease," said Melissa Stokes, a freshman majoring in nursing at SSU.

[A quote should stand alone in its own paragraph and support the paragraph directly before it.]

SSU has been hosting its Healthy Hearts event on Fort Lauderdale Beach since 1987 as a way to support heart disease research and has donated more than $10 million to the American Heart Association over the course of the event's 30-year run. This year's event raised $200,000.

"Sunshine State University is proud to support the American Heart Association in its mission to fight heart disease and stroke," said Charleston Stanton, Ph.D., president of SSU. "The funds raised by our Healthy Hearts event contribute to innovative research and education furthering that mission."

Although all SSU students are encouraged to participate in the event, undergraduate and graduate students from the university's College of Health Sciences are responsible for organizing, programming and staffing the event.

"It's a great experience learning how to plan, promote and execute an event, especially one that is dedicated to saving and improving lives," said Gregory Harper, a senior majoring in biology at SSU.

For more information about Sunshine State University's Healthy Hearts event, visit www.SSUHealthyHearts.com

[The last line of the release should always direct readers to where they can find more information by listing a phone number, email address, URL, social media handle, etc.]

About Sunshine State University (SSU) [Include the organization's boilerplate]

Located in Fort Lauderdale, Florida, Sunshine State University (SSU) is a dynamic, research-driven institution dedicated to providing quality educational programs across a wide range of fields, including law, medicine, business, oceanography, psychology, education, arts, humanities and social sciences. Founded in 1960 and named in homage to the sunshine state, SSU celebrates the state of Florida while preparing its students to live, work and interact in a global society.

####

[#### or -30- signifies end of release]

Other Types of News Releases

By Michael Laderman

To me, as, first and foremost, a writer both at heart and professionally, the cool thing about news releases is that they are all so much the same, and yet, all so very different, in so many ways — all the time.

And so no matter what event it is that you are about to do your news release on, or what person, company or industry that you are charged with focusing on "pitching" [e.g. informing via a news release], no matter what, it must be written.

A common sense statement, perhaps, in a textbook such as this. But, since circa 2010, not so much in the real world, when, all too often, other types of releases are needed and required [for potential promotional success], and the written press release gets tossed by the wayside.

As we delve into these so-called "other types" of releases, e.g. video news releases, social media releases, etc., remember the aforementioned sentence.

"But not so much in the real world, when, all too often, other types of releases are needed and required, and the written press release gets tossed by the wayside."

In other words: The "traditional" press release tends to get lost as the standard bearer of news dissemination when these other types of releases are brought to the forefront.

And they shouldn't. Even as we delve into other "press release options."

So let's keep that in mind, fellow communicators, as we discuss what one should never forget: That there are so many other ways to not only use the traditional release, but also tie them in with the various other release options that are out there today, and that will come about tomorrow. The overriding thought, too, is a definition of what it is we do — that public relations is doing a good job and telling the world about it.

In this ever-changing world of technology in which we live and work, it is not just about *writing* that press release, and making sure that your words are distributed appropriately and properly.

It is also about finding the right distribution channels, and the right means of doing just that. And not just with those words. But with *other words* that drive people to your press release on its specific landing page.

Today, the options to create various forms of press releases are aplenty, be it Facebook, Twitter, Linkedin, Vimeo, YouTube, etc.

From the perspective of a communications leader, I typically and strongly suggest not choosing one over the other. For when not only writing but distributing a press release, you would be remiss to not consider all the different options that are utilized today [whatever *today* is], each and every time.

Press releases, quite frankly, can be the standalone traditional release, or those that are used as a video news release, or a social media release.

From the communicator's perspective, there is not always a right or wrong way to do a release. Again, no "one size fits all" in this business.

As the communications expert here, you are in charge of deciding which ones — either one, or all, or any in-between — as means of dissemination and production you wish to use.

So, do something for me right now. In your head, come up with a product that you already know of — first thing that pops into your head — and come up with an announcement about that product. For example, if a fan of Coca Cola, then pretend you are charged with announcing a new Coke product.

Now, think about what you would do to let not just the media know of it, but the world as a whole.

PS: Always keep in mind, when we say that public relations is doing a good job and telling the world about it, you're really not going to tell the entire world about it. That just means to get the biggest audience that you can possibly get with whatever it is you're doing. And to do that, you have to make sure that you are literally using all the tools at your disposal.

So as of the writing of this chapter — and, from your perspective, the reading of this chapter — let's look at the tools at our disposal.

Social Media Releases

We use social media every day. As such, whether you have realized or not, you see news releases every day in the forms of video clips, and/or social media postings.

If you're on Pinterest, and you see a new product being shown, that technically can be called a social media release.

If you are on Twitter, and you see one of the sponsored ads, and it has 280 characters on there, and there is a link with it to click on for more information [which potentially and, most likely, drives you to even more text with, say, a video and photos attached to it], that is technically a social media release.

When you are on YouTube, and you see a new video announcing a new product, and then, in the text that comes with it, there is a link to more text and additional videography, that, too, is a social media release.

All different, but all the same. They all share the following: Telling you who, what, when, where, why and how. Just like a traditionally written press release.

Again, all things that you have seen and used and have done in your lifetime in just the past 15 years.

Remember I said this is cool? All that said just above, that's the cool part of this.

Video News Releases

Let's cut right to the chase: YouTube, as the hub of video activity on the web, is both a social media platform *and* a search engine. To me, it is the top place to store your VNR. And it is why we mention YouTube among Twitter and Facebook platforms.

A video news release, quite simply, is a press release put into video form. It is done typically by people like me and you. It is put together by public relations professionals as a video in order to simulate an actual news report. It used to be that VNRs would only be sent directly to television stations locally, regionally and/ or nationally with hopes that the station and/or network would either fully run with the video as it were distributed, or that parts of it could be used in an actual news report done by the station itself that picks it up.

Since 2006, specifically, as YouTube really began taking a stronghold on social media, video news releases now had its own separate platform. No longer did a public relations agency or communications expert have to rely on the whim of a producer or assignment editor as to whether or not the video would be used whatsoever. With YouTube, and those like it, that changed the game to where — utilizing the strength of social media, and these skills, ways and means of driving people to the respective landing page — communicators had an additional resource for their message to be seen.

They've come a long way [video news releases] since first they began to be used. Before the internet, they were being sent out via cassettes and DVDs. Full production that came into play took full recording studios, old time graphics and no means whatsoever of adding attachments to it. Old school, indeed.

As society and its technology began growing and getting better, CDs and DVDs were the name of the game.

Thank goodness for the growth of the internet and social media. When the days of Facebook, Twitter, LinkedIn and Instagram began growing and expanding, VNRs and, hence, social media releases grew right along with them.

Thanks to our smartphones, anybody can do a video news release right now. Many of you might be doing one right now in the form of a blog. Turn it into a release, make an announcement, say something cool. Put it out for the world to see. Give them the opportunity to view it. That is a video news release.

But I always go back to my subjective fact: You must always include text and written copy with what you were doing.

So, let's check this out. Here are a few recent things that my public relations agency, 20 A-M COMMUNICATIONS, has done for various clients, including the Blue Bamboo Center for the Arts, Performing Arts Matter, the Caribbean American

Association of Lake County, and saxophonist "Mr. Casual" Charlie DeChant, sax and keyboard player for Daryl Hall and John Oates. All different kinds of people and different kinds of organizations, using all different means of production and distribution. It uses social media. It uses video. And it uses traditional media.

Now, here's a twist when discussing video news releases: The old way of doing video news releases is that they must be an actual news report where it can be picked up and taken as is. That remains to be true. That is not incorrect. I am a strong proponent though, of sending quality video whether in the form of an actual news item or promo piece to news organizations — because they will be able to edit the audio and the video and make it fit as they need.

If you are pitching somebody as an expert, such as another client, Patrick Crews [PHC Counseling Services], then you will be best to do away with the audio or background music and the pretty graphics that you would typically include in a regular promo video. Otherwise, send your written text along with the video with the social media post. Not just one or the other.

Which goes directly back to the first points we made together: Do not toss to the wayside the traditional written press release or similarly written text. Because as you will now see, the written release and/or pitch goes hand-in-hand with both the social media release and the video news release.

They can be done individually, but why would you do such a thing?

Let's look at the social media release right now. Let's say that you've done the best-ever video news release. You have video. You have a press release. And you have a landing page. Essentially, you're ready to send something out.

How do you post it? How do you make it to where people actually know it is a news item that they should not only view and read, but can feel free to use, in fact you are encouraging them to use? That's where the style comes into play. That's where knowing the difference between running social media for you or your family, on a personal level, is completely different than doing it on a professional level.

Again, totally subjective.

But how I do this, and how I have been continuing to do this, has been working very well for me and my teams for 15 years. I do not buy into the other experts whose different opinions encourage the use of little to no text [e.g. written verbiage] to go along with their social media post. I do not buy into the means and ways of just letting the post itself do all the talking, and in a sense, the selling of my press release.

Telling a story is not just video. It's not just social media. To me, it has to also be the written word. It ties in with the reasons that I still feel, after all these years of professional successful experiences, that there is no better way to get the word out about a product or service you offer than one-to-one, person-to-person, face-to-face, handing somebody something literally in their hand.

"Traditional" works.

If I did a two-minute video, and it was the greatest video in the world, and sent it out to 1,000 people, of those 1,000, I'd be lucky if 20% click the link. Of that 20%, of those 200, I'd be lucky if 40% watched at least a minute of that 40% of that 20%. Of those 1,000, I would be lucky if 5% watched anywhere from three seconds to 10 seconds of my promo video. I would be lucky if 1% of that 1,000 watched the video all the way through, beginning to end.

All this, again, knowing that the best video in the world has everything that they're going to need to know about my product or my service. It has the who, what, when, where, why and how. It has graphics. It has contact information. It has great imagery.

But if only 1% of 1,000 are going to watch it, then I still contend that face-to-face, hand-to-hand, person-to-person is the way to go.

So how do you beat those odds? You make sure that your words with your social media post and with your video post are strong enough that they, themselves, help to tell and share the story of which you want them to view. Please don't just say, "click here for awesome news release." Or "don't miss this great video." Or, "you're making a mistake for not clicking the link."

Ask yourself this. When you see just a one or two sentence directive of "click now," or "don't miss this," how often do you typically click on it? If you're anything like me, it takes more than just suggestive selling for me to click the link. And I assure you; it takes more than just suggestive selling for news, individuals and outlets to click *your* link. You'd better sell your video and social media post by telling a story.

It's funny, I have been told by other experts — specifically those who are "experts" in search engine optimization — that little to no text with video and/or social media releases are the way to go. And yet, in head-to-head comparisons, those with more verbiage consistently garnered higher social media engagement rates than those with little to no text.

In this subjective world of media relations and communications, do what you feel to be best. Change when you *need* to change and when you *should* change. But when you know something's working, stick with it.

And telling one's story — via the written word — is what has consistently provided positive results for me, for years. It is why I encourage you to utilize your news release writing skills when developing your social and video news releases.

Follow the basic steps of telling a story. Follow the basic news release style, in which you have incorporated the who, what, when, where, why and how, and place those strategically in your posts.

Then develop your social media and video news release, combine your select text, and watch it take off. Use them all together to help promote your product and services that you are pitching, and more often than not, you and your clients will find the successes that you are hoping to gain.

Exercises

Exercise 2.1 – News Release

You are the public relations representative for Sunshine State High School, and you need to issue a news release for an upcoming event. Using the information below, craft a news release with the template included with this chapter. Remember to apply AP Style and inverted pyramid to your writing. Use Miami, Florida, as your dateline and November 6, 2020, as the release date. The headline should be in Downstyle. All names/proper nouns are spelled correctly.

Who: Sunshine State High School (SSHS) administrators and students; Miami affiliate of the National Career Development Association (NCDA)

What: "Career Development Day"

When: Friday, Nov. 13, 2020

Where: Sunshine State High School in Miami, Florida

Why: Sunshine State High School has partnered with the local affiliate of the National Career Development Association to host "Career Development Day" as part of National Career Development month in November.

Additional information:

- Sunshine State High School Principal Sheila Warren has been working with NCDA since early 2020 to develop the idea for "Career Development Day" and offer students a series of professional development and career-driven workshops.
- Quote from Warren: "It's important that our students be exposed to career development skills now, especially our juniors and seniors who are preparing to graduate and enter college. We want them to be as prepared and professional as possible in achieving their future career paths."
- During the event, NCDA representatives will host workshops on resume writing, dressing for success, interviewing skills and more.
- Quote from Anthony Fox, president of the NCDA Miami affiliate: "We are honored to partner with Sunshine State High School for this exciting event exposing high school students to career development skills. From resume writing to dressing for success, our workshops are designed to help these students prepare for their future careers."
- The event will take place on the SSHS Miami campus from 9 a.m. to 2 p.m.
- Boilerplate for SSHS: Sunshine State High School (SSHS) is based in Miami, Florida, and is a private, four-year secondary school committed to ensuring that all students receive a quality education, within a safe, diverse and multidisciplinary learning environment. SSHS is home to more than 2,000 students spanning grades nine through 12. Its mission is to prepare its students to live, work and interact in a global society.
- As part of the event, the NCDA is hosting an essay contest open to all SSHS students. Students will be asked to submit a 500-word essay on why they think dressing professionally is vital to success. The NCDA will announce the winner during the event and will award the student with a $2,500 college scholarship.
- For more information about "Career Development Day" at SSHS, email Career DevelopmentDay@SSHS.edu or visit www.sshs.edu/career developmentday
- The event will also feature a Career Expo from 1–2 p.m. that showcases real professionals from different fields who will discuss their respective professions with students.

Exercise 2.2 – AP Style Skill Drill

Locate 10 AP Style errors in the news release below. Correct the errors using AP Style editing symbols.

SUNSHINE STATE UNIVERSITY

FOR IMMEDIATE RELEASE
August 27, 2020

Media Contact:
John Smith
(555) 555–5555
firstlast@SSHS.edu

Sunshine State University Names Elizabeth Keystone, Ed.D., as vice President of Academic Affairs

FORT LAUDERDALE — On Monday, Aug. 27, Sunshine State University named Elizabeth Keystone, Ed.D., as its new vice president of Academic Affairs.

"We are delighted to welcome Dr. Keystone to SSU" said SSU President Charleston Stanton, Ph.D. "SSU will greatly benefit from her wealth of knowledge and experience in student affairs."

For the last 20 years, Keystone has served as the director of student affairs for SFU. Prior to that, she served as an associate professor of education for SSU's College of Education.

"I am excited to join the Sunshine State University community," Keystone exclaimed. "I look forward to meeting and working with many of SSU's students to give them the best college experience possible."

Keystone will serve as one of five vice presidents for SSU. The SSU administration will formally introduce her to the student body during its back-to-school assembly on Wed., Aug. 30.

Elizabeth holds a doctorate in education from South Florida University (SFU). She also earned a master's degree in higher education and a bachelor's degree in elementary education from SFU.

For more information about Keystone and her role with SSU, visit www.ssu.edu/news

Sunshine State University (SSU)

Located in Fort Lauderdale, Florida, Sunshine State University (NSU) is a dynamic, research-driven institution dedicated to providing quality educational programs across a wide range of fields, including law, medicine, business, oceanography, psychology, education, arts, humanities and social sciences. Founded in 1960 and named in homage to the sunshine state, SSU celebrates the state of Florida while preparing its students to live, work and interact in a global society.

####

Exercise 2.3 – Social Media Releases and Video News Releases

Go back to your previous news release assignment and write actual text for social media releases and video news releases.

For your social media release, do one for Facebook and one for Twitter.

Tip: Start long, then trim. Just like we have talked before; everything starts out as a full press release — whether in reality, or in your head. Get all the information out in front of you that you will need. It is more often easier to cut copy then to add copy.

So, since you have unlimited carte blanche space on Facebook to write what you want and need to write about, start with your Facebook post. Keep to the facts on the post [e.g. who, what, when, where, why] and include a call to action.

For Twitter, remember: You've got only 280 characters, so make them count. And in those characters, don't forget to include your call to action.

For a video news release: Put yourself in the shoes of a TV or web producer. What would they want to receive? This VNR assignment is twofold: First, write a script for how your VNR would appear once complete. Then, write your text that you would include with your VNR on YouTube. [Reminder: It's pretty much a press release, give or take a few paragraphs — but that's your call.]

Chapter 3

Media Pitches

Whitney Lehmann

Purpose

Along with news releases, media advisories, news and feature stories, media kits and others, pitches are another tool that public relations professionals have in their "tool box" that can be used to garner media coverage for an organization. Pitches can take many forms — in-person, through a phone call, by email and even through social media.

> A pitch is a strategic message that attempts to persuade an individual journalist or blogger to write the story described in the pitch. A pitch—whether an e-mail, phone call or social media message through a website such as LinkedIn— promotes, or 'pitches,' a story idea.
>
> (Marsh, Guth, & Poovey Short, 2012, p. 65)

Pitches invite specific members of the media to cover a client in a certain way. This could be inviting them to cover your client through photography (called a photo opportunity or "photo op"); through a TV broadcast; through radio interviews; through a news or feature story; or even through social media (e.g., blog posts).

Whereas news releases are written ready for publication, and sometimes are published word-for-word, pitches are not.

"In a pitch, as opposed to a feature news release, the story isn't yet written — so a journalist or blogger can feel a stronger sense of ownership of the potential story" (Marsh, Guth, & Poovey Short, 2012, p. 65).

Unlike news releases and media advisories, pitches are not written in third person; they are personalized and conversational and, therefore, are written from a second person point of view — the "you" perspective.

Targeted and Personalized

In addition to being specific about the type of coverage sought, pitches target specific members of the media.

"The objective is to contact journalists and bloggers on a one-to-one basis and convince them that you have a newsworthy story or idea" (Wilcox, Cameron & Reber, 2016, p. 256).

For example, a photo op would be pitched to a photo editor; a radio interview would be pitched to a program director; a news or feature story would be pitched to an assignment editor; social media content would be pitched to a blogger or social influencer; and so on.

"The last thing any journalist wants to receive is an auto-generated message that is being pitched in the same manner to everyone on a media list," (Belicove, 2003, para. 13).

The opportunity for coverage, AKA the "pitch," is tailored specifically to the journalist, his or her media outlet and his or her "beat" (reporting specialty). For example, let's say you are a publicist who represents a celebrity chef who is about to launch her own cooking show on a national TV network. As the publicist, you may pitch a news or feature article to the editor of a popular culinary magazine, to a reporter who regularly writes for the food section of a national newspaper, to the producer of a morning TV show that regularly features live cooking segments, to a widely followed food blogger, to a social media influencer with millions of foodie followers, and others.

Pitches are also *personalized* and should address the person by name, mention his or her media outlet, beat and previous work.

> Pitching is a fine art, however, and public relations personnel must first do some basic research about the publication or broadcast that they want to contact. It's important to know the kinds of stories that a publication usually publishes or what kind of guests appear on a particular talk show. Knowing a journalist's beat and the kinds of stories he or she has written in the past is also helpful.
> (Wilcox, Cameron, & Reber, 2016, p. 257)

News "Hook" or Angle

In addition to being targeted and personalized, successful pitches have a "hook" or news angle that appeals to the media. They are *newsworthy* and offer news value. "Getting the attention of media gatekeepers is difficult because they receive literally thousands of news releases and media kits every week. So, the major question is how to get your story noticed among a dense forest of news releases" (Wilcox, Cameron & Reber, 2016, p. 256).

PBS (What is Newsworthy?, n.d.) outlines five news values to describe "what's newsworthy":

1. *Timeliness* – "Immediate, current information and events."
2. *Proximity* – "Local information and events."
3. *Conflict and Controversy* – "When violence strikes or when people argue about actions, events, ideas or policies."
4. *Human Interest* – "Unusual stories of people who accomplish amazing feats or handle a life crisis."
5. *Relevance* – "People are attracted to information that helps them make good decisions. If you like to cook, you find recipes relevant. If you're looking for a job, the business news is relevant."

In addition to the above, newsworthiness could include making your organization part of a "bigger-picture" story. This could mean tying your organization to the growth of a specific industry, to the popularity of a certain trend or even to a hot-button topic. For example, an organization preparing to host a female empowerment event in response to the widely covered #MeToo movement would be considered newsworthy as part of this "bigger story" that is now taking place globally.

Regina Luttrel and Luke Capizzo (2019), referencing a model of media relations developed by public relations scholars Lynn Zoch and Juan-Carlos Molleda (2006), describe news value as an "information subsidy" or "value of content within a particular pitch made by a public relations professional to a journalist" (p. 8).

"It could include access to a difficult-to-reach source, a head start on information not yet available to the public, or details about a particular situation not shared with other media outlets" (Luttrell & Capizzo, 2019, p. 8).

Pitches can also be *exclusive*, meaning the story is offered exclusively to a specific media outlet. "The media like exclusivity—getting a story idea that no other publication is getting at that time and being the first to publish such a story. Consider your goals and target audience first and select a publication that greatly influences or is widely read by that group" (Zappala & Carden, 2010, p. 123).

Check out the "Perspective from the Pros" feature below for more tips on what makes a newsworthy — and successful — pitch.

❖ PERSPECTIVE FROM THE PROS

By Heidi Carr

Pitching is probably the most difficult thing a PR practitioner has to do — but the rewards are worth all the angst. What makes it so challenging?

1) You have to come up with a really interesting story to pitch, AND
2) You have to tailor your pitch for one specific member of the media.

As an editor, I received nearly 1,000 pitches a week and probably picked one or two to work with.

Why did so many pitches end up in the proverbial circular file?

Mostly, the PR person was pitching what the client wanted her or him to pitch, which wasn't a very interesting idea. It's your job to put a twist on it and make it an experience the journalist can't resist.

Any story a reporter accepts has to have several of the following criteria:

1. Location: It's of interest to their market audience.
2. Timeliness: It's just about to happen or has just happened.

3. Me-too: It's a story people can relate to.
4. Uniqueness: It's really bizarre.
5. Controversy: It's full of conflict.
6. Star power: It's got a celebrity involved.

Let's take your client, the owner of a gourmet doughnut shop. She wants you to promote the opening of a new shop in another part of the city. An editor getting a pitch that invited him to the opening of the new shop would think "Big deal. Why would anyone care about a new doughnut shop opening up?"

What can we do to make the story idea more appealing? And which of our six criteria does our story idea fulfill?

1. The new store is located in the market area of the journalist's publication. ✓
2. The store is about to open. If you're smart, you can get a story published before it opens or get the reporter there for the opening. ✓
3. Who doesn't like doughnuts? But do people really know what goes into making them? What if you arranged for the reporter and videographer to come to the store at 4:30 a.m. and get their hands in the brioche. This could result in a fun story about all the work that goes into those gourmet doughnuts while the rest of the world is asleep. Viewers would get to see people literally rolling in the dough. ✓
4. Your doughnut store is famous for having bizarre flavors, like maple and bacon, and white chocolate très leches. Consider having a special flavor that will only be served on opening day. If a doughnut connoisseur wants to try a passion fruit and mango brioche glazed in a red dragon fruit glaze and topped with fresh slices of dragon fruit and mango, there is only one place that will have it and for a very limited time. ✓
5. You won't want to publicize anything negative about doughnuts, like their calorie count, so let's not focus on that kind of conflict. But we can create a positive kind of conflict in the form of a competition. Promote a contest where the viewers choose the new flavor. They can cast their votes via a social media contest, which potentially could get thousands of people involved. ✓
6. You arrange for a local celebrity to be at the store opening. Imagine someone like Dwyane Wade holding up two doughnuts like glasses in front of his eyes and mugging it up for the camera. I've always found people really game to be part of a fun story, and Dwyane loves donuts. (Besides, he'll burn off those 650 calories in about 10 minutes of practice). ✓

TIMING IS EVERYTHING

To me, there are three different kinds of pitches:
- pre-event
- live event coverage, and
- evergreens

Your client will always give you events they want covered, but for my money, you'd be smarter to pitch evergreens. A lot of these stories are right under your nose, and the advantage is the reporter can come out any time to cover it, and if breaking news happens and your story gets bumped, your "evergreen" story has a longer shelf life.

Event coverage is the easiest to cover, but these can annoy the audience if they're finding out about a really cool thing to do after it has happened. On the other hand, pre-event coverage will get people to the event, but you have to be really creative in coming up with an idea.

Remember the doughnut shop opening?

If you arrange for the reporter to do an "evergreen" story on all the funky flavors the shop offers and the new dragon and passion fruit flavor that will debut at the store's opening, you may just get hundreds of people showing up to try their first ever "Passionate Dragon." *Yummmmmmmm.*

EVENTS
PRE-EVENT COVERAGE

The Advantages
- Makes the public aware about something so they can attend (buy tickets in advance)
- Gets results for the client

The Negatives
- Can be much harder to think of an idea to pitch
- Must be planned and executed far in advance
- Can be very hard to find visuals or people to interview

EVENT COVERAGE

The Advantages
- Relatively easy to cover — there are plenty of visuals and people to interview

The Negatives
- Public finds out about the event after it took place — it annoys the viewer, who may have wanted to take part but it's too late.
- May not help the organization with its goal of getting people involved
- Story may not air or be published if there is breaking news. By the next news cycle, the story will be old.
- With smaller staffs at newspapers and TV stations, there may not be a reporter available at the time the event is happening.

EVERGREENS

The Advantages
- Stories can be published at any point over several news cycles.
- The reporter can work over a period of time, which may result in a very nice "package" with lots of visuals. These stories are often very well written and presented.
- These stories are often "right under our nose," making it relatively easy to get interviews and quotes. They also often have a high popularity with audiences who can relate to them.
- These stories can have a huge impact for the organization when it comes to getting people involved by donating, participating, volunteering, etc.

The Negatives
- None

Structure

While pitches can take many forms (mentioned above), the most popular, and preferred method by journalists, is by email in written form (Marsh, Guth, & Poovey Short, 2012; Wilcox, Cameron, & Reber, 2016).

A PR professor whom I shadowed during graduate school created a fool-proof "formula" to crafting email pitches that I continue to use as a guide today (thanks, Dr. Scott!). This five-part formula includes the following elements: Opening, Connection, Pitch, Details and Closing. Let's take a look at each component.

Opening

Your opening is your salutation/greeting and should be personal to you and your style, but also professional. "Hi," "Hello," "Greetings," are popular choices. Typically, with media pitches, you simply state the person's first name:

"Hi Susan," "Hello Susan," "Greetings Susan," etc.

As directed by the AP Stylebook, we do not use courtesy titles, such as Mr., Mrs., Miss or Ms. (See "courtesy titles" in your AP Stylebook for more guidance on this).

Connection

First, introduce yourself and state your title and organization.

"My name is Colton Chambers, and I'm a public relations manager for the Palms Hotel and Spa in Los Angeles, California."

Now that you've identified yourself, you need to make your connection to the media member your pitch is targeted at. How do you know the writer/editor?

For example, *"We met in August at the hotel's grand opening event."*

Or perhaps you've never met or interacted with this particular member of the media. That's ok, too. You can still make a "connection" — in this case, why the journalist might be interested in covering your story.

For example, *"I follow your 'Luxe Living' column in The Good Life magazine, and I know you often cover unique and trendy spa treatments, such as last month's column on chakra treatments."*

As mentioned above, pitches should be personalized, and they should indicate to the writer or editor that you are familiar with his or her work.

Pitch

The pitch is your news hook and the specific type of coverage you are offering the journalist. Begin with what's newsworthy about your story/pitch.

For example, *"This May, the Palms Hotel and Spa will add dry salt therapy to its list of offered spa services. A hot health trend among celebrities in 2019, salt therapy is quickly becoming the 'must-have' spa treatment for the spring due it its antibacterial and anti-inflammatory properties. The $200 25-minute salt-therapy sessions will take place in a state-of-the-art salt therapy room designed by the Palms' Creative Director Nina Rossum."*

Now that you've identified the news hook, describe the experience are you offering the journalist.

"The Palms Hotel and Spa invites you to tour and experience its new, state-of-the-art salt room first-hand before it opens to the public this May. Rossum and Spa Director Shawn Wood will be available for one-on-one interviews. Photo opportunities will include the unique design of the beautiful and spacious room with its Himalayan salt walls, as well as the full spa and its other amenities."

Details

Once you've stated your pitch, include any relevant details, such as location, dates, times, how to RSVP (if applicable), etc.

Select members of the media are invited to take part in this exclusive first-look and spa treatment at the Palms Hotel and Spa on Monday, April 1, from 1–2 p.m. A tour of the spa and salt room will take place from 1-1:30 p.m., and the complimentary 25-minute dry salt session will follow.

Members of the media should RSVP to me by Monday, March 25, to participate.

Closing

Now that the "pitch" and its details have been covered, direct the journalist to where he or she can find more information about the topic.

For example, *"Additional information about the Palms Spa and its facilities, including the its new salt room, as well as directions to the spa, are included in the attached news release. To view a list of all offered spa services, visit www.thepalmshotel.com/spa/services"*

Next, let the journalist know how you plan to follow up. This follow-up can be "soft" or "hard" depending on your pitching style.

A soft follow-up leaves the ball in the journalist's court. For example, *"If you have any questions, feel free to email me or call me at my number below."*

A hard follow-up, on the other hand, states that you plan to follow up. A hard follow-up might read, *"I will be in touch next week to follow up and answer any questions you may have. I look forward to speaking with you then."*

Finally, conclude your pitch with a signature signoff. "Best," "Best wishes," "Sincerely, "Cheers" and "Thanks," are common choices.

Cheers,
Colton Chambers
Public Relations Manager
The Palms Hotel and Spa
colton.chambers@thepalmshotel.com
555-555-5555

❖ PERSPECTIVE FROM THE PROS

By Michael Laderman

I can't say this enough: Don't be a car salesman.

With whatever you're doing — whether the press release or, as discussing now, your pitch — don't be the individual that's overselling it.

To get someone interested in your press release or story idea, though, you've got to pitch it properly. When you do that, when you write your pitch, when you come up with your pitch, by all means do not oversell it. Do not come across in your pitch as though it would be the end of the world if the editor or reporter you are pitching does not read the information you are sending.

Think about the things that not only work for you [to get you to open up, and read, an email], but that you think would work if you were a news-person on the receiving end of your email. Would you really want to be oversold something? Or would you prefer to just get the basics handed to you in a well-written style?

Your pitch is going to be sent to producers, assignment editors, reporters, photographers, city editors, associate editors, etc., and it's also going to be what you put on the top of your social media posts. So, don't make that pitch something that's overly-fluffy. Don't oversell it. Just make it well-written. That's the best thing you could do in order for your pitch that you're putting out there — whether it is a pitch to get someone to open an attached press release, or whether it is a pitch sent out on its own to let somebody know of something. Do it professionally, yet casually. Do it simply, yet properly.

Just don't overthink it. Let the end-user know what they are about to see in a simple, professional and casual manner.

Media Pitch Template

Note: Insert information where items appear in italics. Remove italics formatting before sending your pitch.

Hi *First Name*,

My name is *First Last*, and I am the *title* for *Name of Organization*. I follow your *beat/reporting specialty* in *Name of Publication/Media Outlet*, and I know you often cover *topic-related* stories, such as your recent piece "*Title of article/feature.*"

What's your story idea and why is it newsworthy/of interest to this journalist? In addition to the news hook, include the specific type of coverage you're offering the journalist (e.g., photo op, feature story, radio interview, etc.).

Include additional details about the opportunity here, including location, date(s), time(s), RSVP information and any other relevant details.

Direct the journalist to where he or she can find more information about your story/pitch (news release, website, etc.). Next, state your soft or hard follow-up.

Your signature signoff, (e.g., "Best," "Sincerely," etc.)

First Last
Title
Name of Organization
Email address
Phone Number
Organization's website

Exercises
Exercise 3.1 – Media Pitch

You are the public relations manager for the children's clothing store Kool Kidz, based in Phoenix, Arizona. Kool Kidz has partnered with the Phoenix location of The Salvation Army to host a holiday toy drive benefitting underprivileged children in Maricopa County. Using the facts below, craft a tailored pitch to a journalist/editor at a Phoenix-based media outlet that includes a specific opportunity for coverage. As the public relations manager, you decide what the opportunity for coverage is (e.g., photography, feature story, local broadcast, etc.).

- Kool Kidz is located in Phoenix, Arizona.
- The children's clothing store offers sizes 0 through 6 years.
- Kool Kidz is organizing a holiday toy drive benefitting underprivileged children who take part in programs offered by The Salvation Army.
- Shoppers visiting the Kool Kidz store from now through Dec. 15 can drop off new, unwrapped toys.
- For more information about the Kool Kidz holiday toy drive or to view a full list of suggested gifts, visit www.koolkidz.com/toydrive
- Kool Kidz is open Monday through Saturday, 10 a.m. to 7 p.m.
- The Salvation Army will visit the Kool Kidz store on Dec. 16 at 12 p.m. to fill its trucks with toys and distribute them to families in need.
- The trucks will be decorated with holiday décor.
- Kool Kidz employees will be dressed as "Santa's helpers" and will help load the trucks.
- Andrea Garcia, founder of Kool Kidz, was inspired by similar "fill the trucks" toy drives taking place in Phoenix. She hopes to make this an annual event.
- Garcia will join employees at the Dec. 16 event.
- Kool Kidz is located at 55 E. Washington St., Phoenix, AZ 85004

Exercise 3.2 – Media Lists

You have just been hired as the communications coordinator for Fur-Ever Homes Animal Care and Adoption Center. The center takes in and cares for adoptable dogs and cats that are searching for their "fur-ever" homes. The 5,000 square-foot, two-story space is open to the public and features an indoor park, pet salon and pet boutique.

Your supervisor has tasked you with updating the center's list of media contacts and is interested in gaining national media coverage for the center. Locate media contacts for the categories below and list why these contacts are relevant to the center and could be targeted for future pitches. For each category, include the name of the publication/media outlet, the name of the specific section/beat/segment for the outlet, and the targeted media member (e.g., reporter, editor, producer, etc.).

For example: Kevin Jacobs writes a monthly column called "The Ruff Life" for the national magazine The Pet Gazette and often features unique animal shelters.

- Print: Reporter or editor of a national magazine
- Print: Reporter or editor of a national newspaper
- Broadcast: Producer of a national news or talk show
- Web: Writer for a widely followed blog
- Radio: Program director for a national radio show

References

Belicove, M.E. (2003). 13 Do's and Don'ts When Pitching to The Media. Retrieved from www.forbes.com/sites/mikalbelicove/2013/12/10/13-dos-and-donts-when-pitching-to-the-media/#44219c285095

Kelleher, T. (2018). *Public Relations.* New York, NY: Oxford University Press.

Luttrell, R.M., & Capizzo, L.W. (2019). *Public Relations Campaigns: An Integrated Approach.* Thousand Oaks, CA: SAGE Publications, Inc.

Marsh, C., Guth, D.W., & Poovey Short, B. (2012). *Strategic Writing: Multimedia Writing for Public Relations, Advertising and More.* Upper Saddle River, NJ: Pearson Education, Inc.

PBS Newshour (n.d.). What is newsworthy? Retrieved from www.pbs.org/newshour/extra/app/uploads/2013/11/What-is-Newsworthy-Worksheet.pdf

Wilcox, D.L., Cameron, G.T., & Reber, B.H. (2016). *Public Relations: Strategies and Tactics* (11th ed.). New York, NY: Pearson Education, Inc.

Zappala, J.M., & Carden, A.R. (2010). *Public Relations Writing Worktext: A Practical Guide for the Profession* (3rd ed.). New York, NY: Routledge.

Zoch, L.M., & Molleda, J. (2006). Building a theoretical model of media relations using framing, information subsidies and agenda building. In C.H. Botan & V. Hazleton (Eds.), *Public Relations Theory II* (279–309). Mahwah, NJ: Lawrence Erlbaum.

Chapter 4

Media Advisories/Alerts

Whitney Lehmann

Purpose

Media advisories — also called media alerts — are another tool in the proverbial "toolbox" that public relations professionals can use to secure publicity for an organization. Unlike news releases, which are written for publication (and are sometimes published word-for-word), media advisories are not intended for publication. Like news releases, however, media advisories/alerts are written with a factual tone from a third-person point of view.

> While news releases can provide a starting point for more in-depth stories, many times they give an editor enough information to be published as written, or in some slightly edited or expanded form. In essence, you have already prepared the story for them. Media alerts have a different purpose. Their content is not intended for publication. Instead, media alerts introduce the media to a potential story and invite them to cover it.
>
> (Zappala & Carden, 2010, p.117)

Similar to media pitches, which are also not intended for publication, advisories serve as an invitation to members of the media to cover something specific. They provide the media with the basic information for a potential story that is timely, such as a news conference, special event, photo opportunity or company announcement. They are brief, never more than one page, and simply provide the who, what, where, when and why for the potential story, so that media gatekeepers can decide whether or not their respective media outlets should cover the story idea. Like media pitches, they may also be sent with an accompanying news release.

"Media advisories should outline only very timely news. A journalist should be able to write a short, complete news story from the media advisory alone — or the media advisory should persuade the journalist to attend a newsworthy event" (Marsh, Guth, & Poovey, 2012, p. 62).

❖ PERSPECTIVE FROM THE PROS

By Michael Laderman

Perhaps the most scrutinized writing and form of communications you will ever produce will pertain to alerts and advisories.

As a general rule, you should always understand the importance of fact-checking multiple times to ensure you are not foolhardy with posting online or submitting a press release too quickly before all facts are garnered. That especially rings true for when you will be charged with writing and distributing alerts and advisories on behalf of the organizations and institutions you represent.

Within public relations and overall communications roles, there will be a day and time where you will be asked to *immediately* send out an advisory or alert for *something*.

And, unfortunately, that something can be anything.

Think of all the harsh things you see on the news today, and understand that, at the heart of it all, is typically a communications expert being asked to get the word out quickly.

Whether it is announcing to a university the closures or open status of campus before, during and after a hurricane, to notifying that same campus of an active shooter on-site — and that it is not a drill and that you need to stand down, lock the doors, turn the sound off on your phone, and not talk — a communications expert is the one charged with ensuring speed and accuracy of the alert.

Prepare yourself as best as possible for not just the day that this will happen to you, but the multiple days and times that this will happen to you.

Do not be afraid of this responsibility. Embrace the opportunity to be the voice of a business or campus or institution or individual when a crisis situation occurs.

Twenty-plus years ago, prior to Columbine, many in our field initially balked at the perceived waste of time crisis communication training took out of our days, because shootings and explosions and terrorist attacks and the like just did not happen often, if ever at all.

Since then, and even more so, 9/11, and multiple campus shootings since then — along with the growth of social media, and the means and ways that news is distributed instantly now — it is imperative that you proactively receive the training you need to learn how to write these alerts and advisories.

Understand that you will be in the spotlight if and when those situations occur.

But with the right training and practice, it can — and will — become second nature to you.

Structure

Advisories can be easily identified by their specific structure, which organizes information by a "WHO," "WHAT," "WHERE," "WHEN," and "WHY" (or paragraphs providing background information and context).

"The most common format for media alerts is short, bulleted items rather than long paragraphs. A typical one-page advisory might contain the following elements: a one-line headline, a brief paragraph outlining the story idea or event, some of journalism's five Ws and H, and whom to contact for more information" (Wilcox, Cameron, & Reber, p. 255).

Let's examine each element of a media advisory more closely:

Header: The header of a media advisory typically includes "MEDIA ADVISORY" centered in all caps as its header. The header area may also include the organization's logo.

Headline: Following the header, most advisories include a headline to communicate the news hook. For example, "Farmhouse Foods to host news conference addressing recent egg recall"

Body: The categories of "WHO," "WHAT," "WHERE," "WHEN," and, if included, "WHY," are often written in all caps, although some advisories break this trend as a style preference. Categories can be written in paragraph form with complete sentences, or they can be written as phrases. This, again, is a style preference. What's important, when deciding how to handle these style choices, is consistency.

If a specific person isn't mentioned as part of the news opportunity, the "WHO" can be dropped. As mentioned below, the "WHY" category can also be omitted if this information is communicated in paragraph form instead.

WHO: If the news opportunity involves specific people, name them here with their respective titles (e.g., Megan Mullgrove, CEO of Farmhouse Foods)

WHAT: What is the news opportunity you are inviting the media to? (e.g., Press conference providing updates to recent salmonella outbreak linked to Farmhouse Foods egg recall)

WHERE: Provide the location, including the full address (e.g., Farmhouse Foods Headquarters, 1112 S. Winding Ridge Lane, Auburn, Alabama)

WHEN: State the day of the week, the date and time (e.g., Monday, March 1, 10 a.m.)

WHY: State background information that provides context (e.g., in February, Farmhouse Foods eggs recalled its cage-free large eggs after nearly 100 people had been infected with the strain of Salmonella Enteritidis in Georgia and Alabama. Since then, the outbreak has expanded with 25 more people ill in three more states, according to the Centers for Disease Control and Prevention.)

Background Information: Rather than include a "WHY" category, a media advisory can address the "why" in paragraph form and offer readers important background information to provide context to the news opportunity (see "WHY" above).

Media Contact: The final section of a media advisory includes additional details and a media contact that journalists can RSVP to or contact with questions. For example, "To RSVP for the news conference, call Gary McKinney, vice president of communications, at 555-555-5555 or email him gary.mckinney@farmhousefoods. com"

Media Advisory Template

LOGO
MEDIA ADVISORY
Headline written in Downstyle

WHO:

WHAT:

WHERE:

WHEN:

In one to two paragraphs, state additional information that provides the journalist with context. This section can be written in paragraph form or can be swapped for a "WHY" category.

The final sentence of a media advisory should direct media members to RSVP if required or provide a media contact to whom journalists can address questions.

Exercises

Exercise 4.1 – Media Advisory/Alert

You're the public relations manager for Bay State University in Boston, Massachusetts. Following the recent resignation of the university's long-time president, Susan Kent, a presidential search committee was announced to select a new president. On Monday, Aug. 5, the university will host a press conference to announce Kent's successor.

Using the information below, craft a media advisory inviting members of the media to the press conference.

- In April, Susan Kent announced she was retiring after a 12-year tenure serving as president of the university.
- During her tenure, Bay State University's enrollment grew by 40% to more than 50,000 students and its four-year graduation rate tripled to 60%.
- The news conference will take place at Founders Hall on the university's main campus.
- The announcement will be made by Bay State University Board Member Hugh Duncan.
- The university's address is 555 Bay State Road, Boston, MA 02215.

- The media contact for the event is Lauren Lopez. Her email is lauren.lopez@ baystateuniversity.com and her phone number is 555-555-5555.
- Members of the media who wish to attend should RSVP to Lauren by Friday, Aug. 2.

Exercise 4.2 – AP Style Skill Drill

Locate 10 AP Style errors in the media advisory below. Correct the errors using AP Style editing symbols.

MEDIA ADVISORY

Fur-Ever Homes Adoption Center to host Second Annual Holiday Adoption Event

WHO: Fur-Ever Homes Animal Care and Adoption Center
WHAT: Second Annual Holiday Adoption Event
WHERE: 555 South Loving Lane, Denver, Colorado 80223
WHEN: Saturday, December 5, 10:00 a.m. to 4 p.m.

'Tis the season for adopting! Members of the Denver community are invited to attend Fur-Ever Homes' Second Annual Holiday Adoption Event featuring fun, food, entertainment and adoptable pets! The family friendly event will include information tables, exhibits, a silent auction, dog-training demonstrations and a Q&A session with Priscilla Hastings, Founder and C.E.O. of Fur-Ever Homes.

Fur-Ever Homes Animal Care and Adoption Center takes in and cares for adoptable dogs and cats that are searching for their "fur-ever" homes. The 5000 square-ft., two-story space opened in 2019 and features an indoor park, pet salon and pet boutique.

References

Marsh, C., Guth, D.W., & Poovey Short, B. (2012). *Strategic Writing: Multimedia Writing for Public Relations, Advertising and More.* Upper Saddle River, NJ: Pearson Education, Inc.

Wilcox, D.L., Cameron, G.T., & Reber, B.H. (2016). *Public Relations: Strategies and Tactics* (11th ed.). United States of America: Pearson Education, Inc.

Zappala, J.M., & Carden, A.R. (2010). *Public Relations Writing Worktext: A Practical Guide for the Profession* (3rd ed.). New York, NY: Routledge.

Chapter 5

Public Service Announcements

Michael Laderman

Purpose

Do you remember growing up as a kid, and watching those children's programs that your parents had on in front of you? Do you remember seeing those 30-to-60 second commercials, those that you knew weren't like the typical commercials that you were used to seeing? Do you remember not liking them, because you thought they were boring, because they tried to teach you something?

Yeah, you were being taught something, all right. You were being fed public service announcements — PSAs, if you will — all throughout your childhood, every time you watched a program on PBS.

Back in my day of growing up in the 1970s, we actually had some of the most famous public service announcements on television, from the Native American Indian, telling us not to "keep America beautiful," to Batgirl teaching us about equal pay. From teaching us about foods and that "you are what you eat," to promoting careers with the United States Air Force.

The messaging was sometimes corny, and sometimes amazing. Same for the videography.

But many times, the educational aspect of it all was second to none.

The thought processes that went into these messages and the dissemination of it, at bare minimum, made you stop and think.

And if it didn't, don't worry, because it would play again and again. And again and again.

So went the public service announcements that were on public television, your local PBS stations and also your local cable TV news channels and affiliates. Not like a CNN, but rather like a Selkirk or a Comcast.

You know, the community channels. The ones that you don't watch anymore, because we're too busy watching YouTube, Netflix and Amazon.

And when we're not we're watching the regular TV channels, the places you would find those kinds of commercials so to speak.

But, realistically, public service announcements are now on your Facebook feed in the form of select YouTube ads. They're still there, only not so much right in front of us.

But how often did you actually look at the video itself? And how often did you actually look at not only the video itself, but listen to the words and hear the message?

Because guess what? Every single public service announcement that has been created either on radio or on TV began as something that can be used in print. It began as a script. It began as a story. It began as a written message telling you, the reader and potentially the viewer, precisely why you should be educated on the following topic.

Audience

Keep in mind public service announcements are just that — they are all about education. They are all about educating you and your family and your team on the issues that are surrounding humanity today, whatever that today is.

Public service announcements are not written and produced to sell your product. They are not to pitch your boss, they are not to make people go to an event — unless it is a fundraiser, which charges no money whatsoever.

Because a public service announcement is written and produced for the general public. It is done as a service to the community. And the announcement is provided for free by the media outlet and outlets that will be running it.

Have you seen those filler messages in newspapers? Those that appear next to actual news articles and features, and seem to be out of place because they are not a true story? Probably not, because there is a good chance that you are not reading the newspaper anymore. But if you are from my day [which is not too long ago], or if you still want to actually know what's going on in your community — and understand wholeheartedly that the only way to do that is to literally pick up your local newspaper at least once a week — then you will know and understand. And you will remember seeing all those little spots and fillers, which sometimes look like advertisements. But more often than not look just like a regular news article plugged in, except they're telling you what you can do to help somebody or something, or someone or some way or some organization.

How to properly use your faucet to save the drinking water. How to protect your pets from a storm. Messages telling us to not drink and drive and encouraging us to wear our seatbelt.

They all began as written PSAs.

Whether or not they are created for the TV, or now for the internet, or for the radio, Spotify, or SoundCloud, they are all written first.

Your charge as a communications expert now is to fully place yourself in the shoes of the audience you wish to educate, to understand wholeheartedly that it is your job and your responsibility to come up with not the most creative thing in the world, but potentially, the most educational thing in the world. And to do that, put yourself in the mindset of a teacher or an educator or a professor. And think of how to best get the message across that will make people stop, think, wonder and act on the words that you, yourself, are asking them to act upon.

So how do you do that? What do you, and should you, do first?

Remember to always go back to what the main focus of this textbook is: Writing.

And write it out. Literally write it out.

Don't think of it as though you are writing out a press release. Don't think of a PSA as writing out a script.

When doing this, let the storyteller in you come out as much, if not more so, than in all other aspects of writing in communications. Because with a public service announcement, you are not just providing the who, the what, the when, the why, and, many a time, the how. More often than not, you are going to have to tell a story.

Because a public service announcement should tug on the heartstrings as best as possible.

A public service announcement should make the reader and, of course, potential viewer or listener want to act — not via a call to action as you would with a pitch or a press release, but rather want to act by either donating or, many a time quite simply, just by doing the right thing.

This could certainly be perceived as something very difficult by an inexperienced writer, for multiple reasons that can be as basic as it's not as simple as doing a standard who, what, when, where, why, how release.

Structure and Format

When writing a specific press release, you look to have all of the pertinent information, contact information and even a quote or two from the main people who have something to do with what you are writing about.

So, if we are writing a press release about a nonprofit, having raised monies for a specific event or fundraiser, it would appear along the lines of:

> ORLANDO, Florida – More than 300 people attended The Share My Story Foundation Inc. Annual Fundraising Gala this past Saturday night, helping to raise $1.2 million on behalf of seniors and veterans, the foundation's executive director, Michael Laderman, announced.
>
> The event, held at the Venue on the Lake in Maitland, raised monies for the nonprofit organization, so that seniors and veterans who cannot afford Share My Story services and products can receive them at no cost to them or their families.
>
> "This was a tremendous event, thanks largely to the people in our community who look to make a difference with those who have paved the way for us," Laderman said. "Those monies raised will go directly to more than 2,400 families that have wanted a Share My Story feature for their loved one but could not afford one. This, in itself, will help write, tell, share and preserve their love one's legacies."
>
> For more information or to donate to The Share My Story Foundation Inc., visit www.TheShareMyStoryFoundation.org.

But for a public service announcement, where you are specifically looking to educate and not just inform, that turns your PSA into more of a script. It turns it now into something that becomes more of a tug on the heart strings of the reader or viewer. For example:

> Hundreds of seniors and veterans each day look to leave their life stories with their families, their friends, their loved ones, and their caregivers — while they are still alive. But they, and their families, cannot afford to do so. You, though,

can help. Please donate today to The Share My Story Foundation Inc., a 501(c)(3) nonprofit organization that raises monies specifically to cover costs for seniors and veterans wanting Share My Story services and products for themselves and their families. To donate, please visit www.TheShareMyStoryFoundation.org.

That very same public service announcement, which can easily go in print, can now be turned into anything you want, for example, a PSA for radio stations to promote.

THE SHARE MY STORY FOUNDATION, INC., A 5 0 1 C 3 NONPROFIT ORGANIZATION THAT RAISES MONIES TO COVER ALL COSTS FOR SENIORS AND VETERANS WISHING TO PRESERVE THEIR LIFE STORIES FOR THEIR FAMILIES AND FRIENDS, WILL HOST ITS ANNUAL FREE FUNDRAISING EVENT THIS UPCOMING SATURDAY NIGHT. FOR TICKETS, VISIT W W W – THE SHARE MY STORY FOUNDATION – DOT – ORG.

Note, too, the style that was just used to type that paragraph. Many, if not most, radio stations prefer PSAs to be submitted to them in all capital letters. Very similar to the way that many individuals prefer a speech to be written for them. Turn it into something for radio and do it in the format that radio stations prefer.

Your PSA can be anywhere between 15, 20, 30, 45 or 60 seconds long. Each one using information taken from the initial generic press release/PSA that you wrote. Because remember, nothing happens without that initial PSA being *written*.

So now we take that initial PSA and turn it into a radio your spot and when you do that, listen to the words you type.

Imagine and literally hear how the words will sound, because as you are writing the PSA for radio, you will say it out loud, because you must know how it is going to sound.

The above was listed as a 20-second spot.

For a 15-second PSA, it would be shortened to:

DON'T MISS THE SHARE MY STORY FOUNDATION'S FUNDRAISING EVENT — SATURDAY, NOVEMBER 7, 6 P.M. — TO RAISE MONIES SO THAT SENIORS AND VETERANS RECEIVE SHARE MY STORY PRODUCTS AT NO COST TO THEM. ADMISSION IS FREE. DONATIONS ACCEPTED. VISIT WWW. THESHAREMYSTORYFOUNDATION.ORG FOR TICKETS.

For a 30-second radio spot:

MAKE YOUR PLANS TO ATTEND THE SHARE MY STORY FOUNDATION'S FREE FUNDRAISING EVENT – THIS UPCOMING SATURDAY, NOVEMBER 7, AT 7 P.M. – HELD AT THE VENUE ON THE LAKE IN MAITLAND. DONATIONS WILL BE ACCEPTED TO ASSIST SENIORS AND VETERANS, SO THAT THEY CAN RECEIVE SHARE MY STORY SERVICES AND PRODUCTS AT NO COST TO THEM OR THEIR FAMILIES, SO THAT THEIR STORIES AND LEGACIES CAN BE TOLD, SHARED AND PRESERVED. FOR TICKETS, PLEASE VISIT WWW. THESHAREMYSTORYFOUNDATION.ORG.

As the need for longer spots is required, simply add the more pertinent information to your public service announcement.

So now that you've written it out, you can look to write your script for any video production you'd wish to do with it. Understand that a PSA is no longer just about sending the announcement out to radio and print outlets. It's literally about also creating it into something that can appear on YouTube and the like.

That does not mean then it must be something that can appear on network television. It does not mean that it must have the high-end quality of those commercials and spots that I had mentioned earlier. Thanks to the advent of social media and video sites just like YouTube, any words, just like music, can be put and stored on and as a YouTube video. Even if it's just taking your words and turning those words into a YouTube video and doing a voiceover and putting that on YouTube, that counts.

Always keep in the forefront of your mind that you are not trying to sell a product. For a public service announcement, it is all about education and information that benefits society as a whole.

That is why, for a public service announcement to be accepted for free on various media sites, it must be a free event, itself, and one that pertains directly to the community at large. PSAs are typically made for nonprofit organizations that do wonderful things for the world.

Your public service announcement writing should make somebody act. Your writing should make somebody do good, and want to do good, for the community at-large. Your writing should make a media outlet want to run your public service announcement at no cost to you. Your writing should make somebody want to click on what your post, no matter where you post it, when you post it, how you post it. Your writing can help change the world by helping an organization that does good for the world succeed.

Public Service Announcement Template (Formatted for Radio)

Media Contact:
First Last
Name of Organization
555-555-5555
Email address

Headline should be written in Downstyle, present tense, with a large type size such as 24 point

30-second PSA *Always include length of submitted PSA

> BODY OF THE PSA SHOULD BE IN ALL CAPS. BEGIN, WHEN POSSIBLE, WITH A CALL TO ACTION. AT MINIMUM, ENSURE YOU INCLUDE THE WHO, WHAT, WHEN, WHERE AND WHY. LINE SPACING SHOULD BE 1.5, AND FONT SIZE SHOULD BE AT LEAST 14 POINT. USE A BASIC FONT, SUCH AS TIMES NEW ROMAN.

Exercises

Exercise 5.1 – Public Service Announcement

Select a non-profit event that is happening in the future, in your hometown. Research it and then write a public service announcement — for print.

Once your print announcement is written, turn that into four radio spots: 15, 30, 45 and 60-second spots.

Then, take your 30-second spot and turn it into a YouTube video. [Keeping in mind: No actual video footage is needed. It can technically be just a promotional image or flier of the event you are promoting, simply with a voiceover, i.e. the radio PSA].

Exercise 5.2 – AP Style Skill Drill

Locate five errors in the public service announcement below related to Associated Press Style. Correct the errors using AP Style Editing Symbols. Note: The PSA is written for print.

Did you know that 1 out of every 4 car accidents in the United States is caused by texting and driving? According to the National Safety Council, nearly 400,000 injuries occur each year from accidents caused by texting & driving. Join millions in taking the pledge to drive distraction free and help make the world a safer place. Visit www.safedriversunite.com to take the pledge today and become an advocate for distraction-free driving.

References

1970s PSAs. Retrieved from www.youtube.com/watch?v=Is5vIf7nwsU&list=PLVvqVg eyKP761vM9PgACeMmhcCdNVfKR_&index=10&t=0s

The Crying Indian – full commercial – Keep America Beautiful. Retrieved from www.youtube.com/watch?v=j7OHG7tHrNM

PSA Short: Time for Timer – "You Are What You Eat" (1970s-1080p). Retrieved from www.youtube.com/watch?v=4EHEvssnMYE&list=PLVvqVgeyKP761vM9PgACeM mhcCdNVfKR_&index=21&t=0s

US Air Force PSA. Retrieved from www.youtube.com/watch?v=qtNPVvYGLTk&list=P LVvqVgeyKP761vM9PgACeMmhcCdNVfKR_&index=24&t=0s

Chapter 6

Media Kits

Whitney Lehmann

Purpose

While media kits are not technically a form of public relations writing, they do involve — and contain — forms of public relations writing, most of which are explored in this text.

So, what then are media kits? *Media kits*, also known as press kits, are a communications tool — perhaps, the ultimate communications tool — used by public relations professionals to garner publicity for their organizations. Media kits bring together a variety of public relations materials, such as news releases, fact sheets, bio sketches, advisories, imagery, b-roll, product samples and more to provide members of the media with the information they need when covering something specific and newsworthy about an organization.

Media kits are used for special events, distributed during news conferences, created for crisis situations, mailed to targeted media and are kept on hand to assist with basic media inquiries.

> As a public communication practitioner, you are—or will become—well acquainted with media kits. They are a staple in our field. A media kit is a public communication tool used to generate news stories about an organization's newsworthy initiative, campaign, special event, major-announcement news conference, product launch, or trade show. It provides the media with the research, facts, perspectives, and historical context that they need to understand in order write about an event or announcement.
>
> (Diggs-Brown, 2013, p. 57)

Media kits provide the media with more information than what's provided to them in a news release. By incorporating a variety of public relations materials, media kits can paint a fuller picture of a topic than one PR material can on its own.

The different types of materials included in a media kit can also change the user experience by engaging more of the senses. For example, let's say you are the public relations director for a health foods company that's launching a new line of almond butter snack bars. A media kit box created for health bloggers and journalists might contain product samples (taste, touch and smell), a fact sheet or brochure listing ingredients (sight and touch) and a USB containing an informational video introducing the bars (sight and sound).

Format

As mentioned above, media kits exist in different formats. A traditional print media kit typically consists of an organization's branded folder with its logo and has inside pockets to hold print materials, such as news releases, fact sheets, back-grounders, bio sketches, advisories and business cards of PR contacts. A digital media kit might exist as a portable flash drive/USB that contains a variety of files, including .pdf print materials and photo and video files, or as an online press room with clickable, downloadable files. Depending on their purpose, media kits can also be creative and out-of-the-box. For example, they can be formatted as social media apps, interactive infographics or as a branded box with product samples and swag.

The format — and contents of — a media kit should be strategic and designed for the particular medium(s) being targeted.

> Traditionally, the contents of the kits have varied based on their use, but the contents are always prepared with the medium in mind. For example, black-and-white glossy photographs that might be useful to print media are not included in broadcast media kits. Sound on CDs that might be in radio news kits are not included in television news kits, which might have videos on DVDs or another digital medium.
>
> (Newsom & Haynes, 2014, p. 162)

The contents of a media kit should also clearly speak to the specific subject matter being promoted. Public relations professionals should begin building a media kit with a news release that communicates the news item with great detail. They can then strategically supplement the news release with additional print and/or digital materials to tell a complete, consistent story.

"A successful media kit generally focuses on one core news story, which is reported in the news release. All other elements of the media kit — background-ers, fact sheets and anything else — support that core news story" (Marsh, Guth, & Poovey Short, 2012, p. 76).

Structure

While media kits can take many different formats, the standard elements of a media kit typically include (Newsom & Haynes, 2014; Zappala & Carden, 2010):

- A news release detailing the news item (e.g., upcoming event, new product or service).
- Background materials providing facts, statistics and historical context (e.g., backgrounders, fact sheets, timelines, organizational charts, infographics, etc.).
- Bio sketches and headshots of key people from the organization, specifically those associated with the news item.
- Contact information, including names and titles of individuals who media members can contact for media inquiries, customer service and investor relations.

While the above elements are standard, additional components may be included depending on the purpose, objective and the medium(s) targeted. Supplemental elements might include (Diggs-Brown, 2013; Newsom & Haynes, 2014):

- Downloadable logos and images associated with the news item, typically with options in both low resolution (used mainly for the Web) and high-resolution (used mainly for print).
- B-roll video footage that can be used by broadcast media.
- A feature story, or human-interest story, related to the news item/subject of the media kit.
- Publications produced by the organization, such as magazines, brochures or newsletters.
- List of sponsors or partnerships associated with the news item (e.g., sponsors of an event).
- The most recent annual report for the organization.
- Calendar of events for the organization.
- Position papers on current issues.
- Financial information, such as earnings releases, financial highlights, stock charts and dividends history.
- SEC (Securities and Exchange Commission) filings.
- And more!

Media kits will often contain a letter outlining the contents of the kit, so that media members can easily navigate them. Media kits that are mailed usually contain a cover letter that explains the purpose of the kit, details its contents and provides contact information for the public relations staff members who can be contacted with questions.

❖ PERSPECTIVE FROM THE PROS

By Whitney Lehmann

During my time working in journalism and public relations, I've both received and produced the gamut of media kits: the formal corporate folder containing a printed news release, fact sheet, backgrounder and bio sketch; the portable flash drive that equips a reporter on deadline with an easy-to-access arsenal of images and PR materials; the branded box containing product samples, swag and flashy marketing materials; the fancy and visually appealing landing page with a custom URL to house a press room featuring b-roll, video recaps, galleries of images, branded hashtags and clickable materials; and so on.

Whether they be traditional or trendy or exist in print or in cyberspace, what I've realized about media kits is that the best media kits best serve the needs of the person or public they're created for. While a print media kit might be appropriate for members of the media who are sitting comfortably in an auditorium for a speaker event, this same hefty folder filled with various documents may not be as appreciated by a reporter who is on his or her feet covering a story with a tape recorder and/or reporter's notepad already in hand — for example, a reporter on site covering a charity 5K race. As a former journalist myself, I can promise you this person does not want to also carry an overflowing folder while he or she literally "chases" the story.

In 2016, as a member of the public relations team for Seminole Hard Rock Hotel & Casino in Hollywood, Florida, we kept the needs of our audience in mind when we created a media kit for the resort's participation in the 2016 Food Network & Cooking Channel South Beach Wine and Food Festival. The festival, which takes place in the silky white sands of Miami Beach, was also not a folder-friendly event. Instead, we ordered custom USBs shaped like guitars with our logo and pre-loaded them with our news releases, fact sheets for our participating restaurants, bio sketches and high-res head shots for our featured chefs, and a gallery of images showcasing the resort's signature dishes and craft cocktails that festival goers could experience at our booth in SOBE's Grand Tasting Village.

Our no-fuss, space-saving media kits were a SOBE success. They allowed members of the media to be hands-free and fully present while sampling our dishes, sipping our cocktails, and engaging in conversation with us about our brand. Bloggers and journalists were also sent home with a small piece of Seminole Hard Rock Hollywood that would serve as a subtle reminder for stories to come.

Exercises

Exercise 6.1 – Media Kit Example

Locate an existing media kit for an organization and review its contents. Write a memo to your instructor that answers the questions below. Use today's date and "Media Kit Example" as the subject. Print and initial the memo and prepare to present your media kit and findings in class.

Note: See Chapter 15 for a memo template.

1. What organization and what newsworthy item about the organization is the media kit designed to promote?
2. Who is the specific audience for this media kit? (e.g., health bloggers and journalists, etc.)
3. What format does the media kit take (print, digital, etc.)?
4. What specific components does it include (news release, fact sheet, etc.)?
5. In your opinion, do the chosen format and selected components best communicate the subject matter? Why or why not? What might you do differently?
6. In your opinion, does the media kit best serve its audience? Why or why not?

Exercise 6.2 – Media Kit for a Client

Work with a student organization or local nonprofit to create a design/plan for a media kit that promotes a newsworthy aspect of the organization. It could be a new product or service, an upcoming event, a new hire, a new initiative, or any other newsworthy piece of information that can be used to garner publicity for your "client."

As the public relations representative, you decide what format the media kit should take and which components it should contain in order to best communicate the information and meet the audience's needs.

In 500 words or less, describe your plan for your proposed media kit. Make sure to include a basic description of the organization and the specific news item being promoted. Submit your plan in memo form (see Chapter 15) and use today's date and "Media Kit Design" as your subject.

References

Diggs-Brown, B. (2013). *The PR Style Guide: Formats for Public Relations Practice* (3rd ed.). Boston, MA: Wadsworth, Cengage Learning.

Marsh, C., Guth, D.W., & Poovey Short, B. (2012). *Strategic Writing: Multimedia Writing for Public Relations, Advertising and More* (3rd ed.). Boston, MA: Wadsworth, Cengage Learning.

Newsom, D., & Haynes, J. (2014). *Public Relations Writing: Form & Style* (10th ed.). Boston, MA: Wadsworth, Cengage Learning.

Storytelling

Chapter 7

Interviewing

Heidi Carr

Who doesn't like to talk about themself?

I don't see any hands raised!

Even better, once you start asking someone questions about a topic they are excited about, almost everyone gets excited to share their knowledge with you.

Interviewing is really quite fun, but there are some tips that will help you get the best results.

Let's take it in sections: Preparing for the interview, the actual interview and after the interview.

Preparation

Let's be honest, sometimes you have time to prepare and sometimes you just gotta jump in. Whether you have five days or five minutes before the interview, there are two things you <u>must</u> do:

1. Research and
2. Prepare Questions

Why do research if you're going to talk to the person who will likely tell you everything you need to know? Because you have to know what to ask and you have to have a basic grasp of what they are talking about.

Your basic research — whether it's looking up articles on the topic, seeing what others have written about the subject or looking at research/data/polls — will put you at a good starting point. But there's much more to do.

Prepare a list of questions. Yes, write them down, group them by topic and practice different ways of asking them. You may not eventually ask every question on your list, but it will be a great reference point when you are in the middle of the interview.

The Interview

First question for you — will this interview be over the phone or in person?

It really depends on the project you are working on. If it's an executive bio, pitch or feature story for the web, it is a million times better to meet face-to-face with the person. If it's for a news release or something much simpler, a phone interview will do. (Facetime and Videochat are fine, too).

Don't even think about conducting an interview via email or text message. There are so many reasons why this is bad, bad, bad:

- It's very easy for the person to miss or avoid a question.
- The person may not understand the question, or the person may write an answer that you don't understand. Then you have a back-and-forth that will take days, if you're lucky. When you are meeting in person, if the person gives you an answer that is lacking, you can ask them to go into more detail right then.
- You send the questions and never hear back.

Your professor, and eventually your boss, will NOT want to hear these words, ever: "I emailed him the questions, but he has not gotten back to me yet."

So don't be shy! Pick up the phone and give your person a call, and if possible, make an appointment to meet them.

What You Gain From Going in Person

Another reason why in-person interviews are best: You get to use *all* your senses.

Speaking: It's not only what you ask, it's how you ask it. Have you ever sent an email that you meant to be friendly and the person was offended? The tone in your voice can put people at ease, even when you are asking tough questions.

Hearing: Listen, listen, listen to what they say. Don't interrupt. It's great to nod your head and utter a soft "uh-hmmm" as encouragement. But let them do the talking.

Smelling: Depending on your topic, the odor may be very relevant. Once you bring up the scent of cinnamon buns fresh out of the oven or the stench of weeks' old garbage in your story, the reader is immediately transported to where you want them to be.

Touching: This may help you add texture to your story. If you are working on a piece about a new cosmetics line, dab a bit of the product on your skin. Does it leave you with a tingle? Or feeling silky smooth?

Tasting: If you are working on a piece involving food, this is a must. If you are going to write a news release about food at the county fair, you need to know how hot the Three-Alarm Buffalo Wings really are, or if chocolate-caramel sandwich cookies taste a little like Oreos. (They don't, they are wayyyy better).

Seeing: Have you ever emailed someone and gotten an image in your head and then when you met, the person was nothing like what you'd envisioned? It's the same exact thing with meeting someone in his or her own environment.

The little details you note — whether they are bustling around or sitting relaxed, whether their office walls are covered with awards and commendations or photos of their dog — will make them become more real in your piece.

Get Out That Notepad

There's lots of technology out there, but be aware that recording a conversation can cause lots of headaches: If the person is soft-spoken, you might not be able to hear them. There's a chance the recorder won't work. Remember, too, sometimes the person you are interviewing will keep looking at the recording device, feeling a little intimidated. And the worst part comes after the interview when it takes you hours to transcribe your recording.

That's where the old-fashioned pen and notepad come in.

The ideal situation is to use both.

Once you get started with the warm-up talk, ask the person if they are comfortable with you recording the interview. Set your recorder between the two of you, but a little to the side so it's not right in their line of sight.

Then get out your list and start with your questions. Take notes by hand, but a journalist's great secret is to just put a time on your notepad when the subject says something brilliant that they know they will use.

Example:

4:30 quote about Afghanistan rescue

(This means the quote you want is about 4½ minutes into your interview. Once you go to write your piece, you'll know exactly where in your recording to go. This trick will save you hours of misery.)

A couple of things to note about recording interviews:

Each state has different rules about recording people without their knowledge. In some states, it is legal as long as one person in the conversation is aware; in others, all parties have to agree to being taped.

If you are interviewing more than one person at once, recording or talking via phone will cause you a headache. It's often impossible to know who is speaking. Group interviews must be done in person (or via the aforementioned Facetime/Videochat).

Asking Questions

Now, about those questions you prepared. Get the ball rolling with a broad question from your list and let the person respond. If the interviewee answers and you don't understand, ask them to clarify. It's better to know for sure than make an assumption later that proves to be wrong.

If what the person is saying is really interesting, ask him to give you an example or go into a little more detail. Don't feel you have to stick with the questions on your list. Use those 5–10 questions as a starting point, but as the conversation unfolds, you may be hearing things that take the interview in a new direction. But if the person is really going off topic, politely steer the interview back by asking another question on your list.

Encourage the person with open-ended questions — avoid yes/no questions, unless it's for emphasis.

Example

Right: Explain to me what led you to write an entire book about road rage.
Wrong: Do you think road rage is a problem?
Right: Governor, are you going to resign from office?

If you do get a rather bland answer, just be quiet. It will make you feel awkward. Nobody likes there to be silence in the room. But if you are quiet, the interviewee will want to fill the void, and will eventually start expounding on the topic.

Go into your project with an idea for an angle but keep your mind open. During the interview, the subject may off-handedly make a comment that you think would make for a more interesting story or a good anecdote in your piece.

Example

Let's say you are interviewing a track coach at a local Boys and Girls Club for a feature story to put on the organization's website. What are some questions you might have put on your pre-interview list?

- What are your goals for the track team?
- In what areas do you think your team is the strongest (hurdles, sprints, marathon, etc.)?
- What's your secret for training these teens during the hot season?
- What's your own track experience?

Now, let's just say that some of the answers the coach gives you are: "The kids who come here come from families that won't be able to afford college tuition. My goal is to get these kids in contention for athletic scholarships, so they can go to a university ..."

"Our kids definitely are among the state's very best in the short-distance sprints. I have two young people—a male and a female—who are both setting records at every meet."

"Yeah, no one likes training when it's 90 degrees out. But it's a lot more painful in the winter when the temperatures never get above freezing. I've seen kids come back after a long-distance run and have icicles forming on their earlobes. But these kids are driven."

"Me? Well, I'm a mid-distance guy. Competed in college in the 1,500 meters and mile run. I nearly made it to the 2008 Olympics—the one in Beijing—but I just missed the cut by a thousandth of a second."

All of those answers could turn into a story — there's no way you could have anticipated the coach just missed the Olympics by a millisecond. Keep the conversation going by asking follow-up questions. Your story will unfold before you.

Ending the Interview

After you've gone through your list of questions — and asked a bunch of new ones — there are a few things you still must do.

Let the person know that you might have more questions and ask them the best way for you to contact them. Get their cell phone number and all the emails they'll give you.

When you go to write your piece, you'll be so glad you have a way of contacting them.

And finally, there's one last thing you absolutely must do: Ask the person you are interviewing for a business card or to spell his or her name. Never assume it's John Smith, it could just as easily be Jon Smythe. And once you get one fact wrong in your piece, you've lost all credibility with your reader.

True story: One of my very first assignments straight out of college was writing a story for a daily newspaper about a local woman who had her recipe chosen as the winner of a national contest. At the end of my interview, I asked the woman to spell her name: "J-A-B-W-O..." she started. I handed her my pen and paper and asked her to print her last name.

The morning the story came out, the woman called me and said she very much enjoyed the story, but I had misspelled her name. "Oh, Mrs. Jabworkowski," I said. "I am so sorry, but I thought that's how you had written your last name on my notepad."

Then came her reply: "Yes, dear, you spelled my last name just fine. But my first name is 'M-A-R-I'."

After the Interview

Transcribe your notes while they are still fresh in your head.

If there is anything that you are reading through that doesn't make sense to you, call the person you interviewed and ask them to go over it again with you. They will appreciate you working to get it right. If you don't understand a topic thoroughly, you can't write about it, even if it's a five-paragraph news release.

Compare what the person told you to what you've found out through your online research. If the person told you that her product is the only one of its kind, do everything you can to verify that.

It's much better that you check out what your subject told you than writing up a pitch and sending it to the media, only to have the reporter do his own research and drop the story because he discovered there are a dozen other products that do the same thing. And once you've lost a reporter's trust, there's no getting it back.

Using Quotes

There are two different ways to incorporate the information you got during your fabulous interview: paraphrasing and direct quotes.

Paraphrasing is when you boil down the information from your source by writing it in your own words but attribute it to the speaker.

Direct quotes are when you use the exact words your source said.

Example

Paraphrase: She will eat anything, even cauliflower, if there is cheese sprinkled on top, Kate said.

Direct quote: "I lick the cheese off Cheetos and put them back in the bag," Kate said. "I will eat anything with cheese on it, even cauliflower."

See the difference? The first one is a simplification of the exact quote. You don't put quote marks around it because it's not exactly what the person said, but the idea is the same.

Why Would You Want to Paraphrase?

- Sometimes your source doesn't speak concisely, or they use jargon. It's up to you to make it easy for your reader to understand.
- You don't want to use a big, long quote. Sometimes it works very nicely to use some of the information you've got paraphrased and then back it up with a pithy quotation that contains nice detail.
- You never want to use quotes from two different people back-to-back. Following up a quote with a paraphrased sentence is a nice transition between speakers.

Fixing Quotes

It is absolutely fine to "fix" a speaker's grammar even when directly quoting them. As long as we are not changing the intent of the sentence, it is acceptable to take out clauses or partial sentences that go nowhere.

Think of it this way: if you were quoting somebody, would you include all the "uhhhhs" they said during the conversation.

We also don't attempt to characterize a person's ethnicity by writing in dialect form — unless it's vital for a story. We never purposely make a person look stupid by including their misuse of a word or bad grammar — unless it is absolutely relevant to the story. We also take out inappropriate language that may have slipped through — again, unless their use of a certain word is the point of the story.

How to Use Punctuation with Quotation Marks

This one stumps a lot of people, even the pros.

The rule is simple: Commas, periods, quotation marks and exclamation marks always go inside the close quote marks. Take a look at these examples:

RIGHT: "I am going to meet my friends for lunch after class," Jake said.
WRONG: "I am going to meet my friends for lunch after class", Jake said.
RIGHT: "Harriet, would you like to join us for lunch?" Jake asked.
WRONG: "Harriet, would you like to join us for lunch"? Jake asked.
RIGHT: "I lost my wallet!" Jake said. "Harriet, will you pay for my lunch?"
WRONG: "I lost my wallet", Jake exclaimed. "Harriet, will you pay for my lunch"?
RIGHT: "Are you cray-cray?" Harriet said. "I'm not paying for your food."
WRONG: "Are you cray-cray"? Harriet said. "I'm not paying for your food".

Also, do not use commas before or after quotation marks if the quotation marks are simply around a song, movie or book title.

RIGHT: Cardi B's breakout album "Bodak Yellow" is No. 1 on the Billboard charts.
WRONG: Cardi B said, "Bodak Yellow" is her best album yet.

Note: When the sentence is a question that contains a title in quotation marks, the punctuation mark goes after the close quote UNLESS the title is a question. Huh? Maybe this will help.
EXAMPLE:

RIGHT: Is there a child who isn't terrified by the Wicked Witch of the West in "The Wizard of Oz"?
ALSO RIGHT: Elizabeth Taylor won an Oscar for her performance in "Who's Afraid of Virginia Woolf?"

Where to Put the Attribution

It's not a hard and fast rule, but usually the speaker's name is given after the first sentence of their quote. Then you can continue on with the rest of their quote. Here's why: You don't want to make the reader have to read all thew way to the end of the paragraph before identifying who is talking.

Very rarely do you want to begin with the speaker's name followed by the quote.

Always identify the speaker with some information that gives the reader an idea of why the person has some expertise on the topic.

Example:

RIGHT: "Last week's heat wave caused a record 12 billion tons of ice to melt in Greenland," said Ted Scambos, a senior researcher at the National Snow and Ice Data Center. "It's the highest single-day total since 1950."

"Is Using 'Said' All the Time Boring?" She Said

This is one area where simplicity wins over creativity. Use the word "said" 99% of the time when quoting someone, whether you are paraphrasing them or quoting them directly.

The reason? It's the quote that should shine, not how the person said it. Once you start changing "said" to announced, believed, revealed, expressed, divulged, noted, made known, proclaimed, recounted, disclosed, articulated, intoned, pronounced, sang, laughed, uttered, vocalized, related, verbalized, voiced, communicated, described, opined, editorialized, whispered, shouted, cried, sobbed, laughed, narrated, recited, hypothesized, reckoned, thought, questioned, queried and the avoid-at-all-cost alleged, you've put the emphasis on the wrong part of the sentence.

Yes, there are exceptions — which is why I gave you that 1 time out of 100 — but if you stick with "said," your writing will be clean. Put the creativity in other parts of your writing.

❖ PERSPECTIVE FROM THE PROS

By Virginia Gil

As a young child, my mother used to call me the question machine. I wanted to know why things happened, how things worked and — once my emotional intelligence kicked in — how certain situations made people feel. My innate curiosity is now less of a nuisance and more of an asset, especially during an interview.

Be inquisitive. Basic interest in your subject is paramount to a good interview. While you won't have an immediate connection with every person you speak with, it's important to find some common ground. Research your subject thoroughly and use it as a launch pad: a deep dive on Google, social media or even public records should inspire you to find out more. After all, optics are only part of the story and a thoughtful interview will help you fill in the blanks.

Determine what kind of listener you are, pay attention and don't be afraid to interrupt. Transcribing interviews is one of the most cumbersome parts of the job but a necessary evil for those without lightning-fast shorthand. I've found that recording cuts the time in half (this only applies to phoners; people aren't as forthcoming when you have a laptop propped open and your digits are producing woodpecker-like sounds). In person, I take notes and jot down time stamps to return to later. Being a tactual listener, I find that writing while listening keeps me more engaged.

The second part to being a good listener is knowing when to interrupt. Politely interject when your subject is meandering or belaboring a point that isn't conducive to your story or furthering your reporting. Guiding your subject isn't rude; rather, it's strategic when done tactfully. Interview fatigue is real, and you don't want your subject to tire out before divulging any real gems.

Allow for silence. Letting the room go quiet makes for an uncomfortable first date, but it's disarming in an interview setting. A few moments of stillness might be what your subject needs to open up. In fact, some of my best quotes have come from the sudden blabbering that ensues after a long, awkward pause. People will overshare if just to fill the dead air — and you want that, so just let it flow.

A successful interview is part first date, part job interview and part social experiment — an intimate exchange where you're trying to be charming, perceptive and aloof all at once. Be present, be flexible and always double check your recorder is on.

Exercise

Exercise 7.1 – Interview Practice

Being able to talk to total strangers on any topic is a skill set that will take you far in any job. But sometimes we have to go outside our comfort levels — way outside — and talk to people who talk differently, think differently, act differently and live differently than we do.

Your task is to go to a location that is out of your comfort zone. No, you can't go as a group, but yes, you can take a friend along for moral support. The "where" will totally depend on your own lack of expertise and curiosity. For example, if you are heterosexual and have never been to a gay bar, you may pick this. If you really hate sports and know nothing at all about football, go to a high school game. If you are a little squeamish with the elderly, go to an assisted living facility, hang out in the lobby and talk to an elderly resident about her life. If you are a diehard Democrat, go to a Republican candidate's speech. If you're not really fond of kids, go to a public swimming pool or playground. If you're afraid of death, go to a public funeral or memorial service.

Find a slice of life you've never experienced and see what it's all about. The main thing is that you get out of your comfort zone and talk to a stranger. Be respectful and honest, but remember, it's about them, not you. Ask them questions and let them talk.

Guidelines:

1. You will write a short story about the place you went and what people were doing there. Use quotes and anecdotes. First names are OK.
2. On another sheet of paper, write a memo to accompany your story. This should include a brief description explaining why you chose the place/experience you chose and what you thought of the experience. Was it different than you expected? Would you ever go back? Were you nervous? Could you relate to the people you talked with on some level?
3. Be sure to use proper AP Style and spelling when writing.

Chapter 8

Background Materials and Backgrounders

Whitney Lehmann

Purpose

Background Materials

Now that you've tackled the art of interviewing, you're ready to start telling your organization's story through background materials.

Background materials are exactly what they sound like — materials that provide journalists with background information on an organization, its people, its products, services or initiatives.

In the Media Relations section of this text, we explored different forms of public relations writing that public relations professionals use to communicate with members of the media, such as news releases, pitches and media advisories. Many times, journalists need more detailed information than what is provided in these materials in order to tell their story. Background materials, such as backgrounders (stay tuned), fact sheets (Chapter 9), bio sketches (Chapter 10) and feature articles (Chapter 12) can help to fill this information gap.

> Once the media respond to your 'new product launch' media alert, for example, they will need more background information on your company and the product to complete their stories. Or, your news release could prompt an invitation from a trade media editor to submit a longer article that shares one of your executive's thoughts on a timely industry subject.
>
> (Zappala & Carden, 2010, p. 132)

Public relations professionals are often charged with creating and updating different types of background materials for an organization to have on file when needed. Background materials can be about the organization, as a whole, or they can also be specific to a person, product, service or initiative.

As mentioned above, background materials often accompany specific types of public relations writing, such as a news release or pitch. For example, let's say a Fortune 500 company is preparing to announce its new CEO. As the company's public relations manager, you might be tasked with crafting and sending a news release to members of the media to announce the new hire. In this situation, including a backgrounder that details the history and mission of the company, as well as a bio sketch that provides additional information about the new CEO beyond what's included in the news release, would be helpful to journalists writing about this news item.

Background materials can also work together to strategically tell a story. For example, let's say an alumnus of a university donated $50 million to his alma mater to create a center for cancer research on the university's main campus. Following a two-year building process, the university is ready to unveil the new center with a ribbon cutting. A public relations professional for the university might be tasked with creating a media kit (Chapter 6) to distribute to journalists at the event that contains a news release announcing the opening of the center; a backgrounder detailing the university's history, mission and vision; a one-page fact sheet for the new center; and a bio sketch about the donor and his extensive background with cancer research.

In addition to supplementing news releases, media pitches and advisories, and being included in media kits for events and news conferences, background materials have many other purposes. They can be posted to an organization's online press room for quick and easy access to journalists needing background information; they can be distributed internally to new employees to acquaint them with the organization; and they can be used as secondary sources for the preparation of brochures, reports and other PR and advertising materials, among other uses.

Process

How does one go about gathering the extensive information needed to create background materials? Use secondary research (Chapter 1) as a starting point and gather all existing information on the topic. Remember, secondary sources can include books, news articles, electronic databases, magazine articles, blog posts, radio interviews, broadcast segments, newsletters, memos, archival records, reference books, fact sheets and other existing background materials, and more.

Next, create a draft of your background material and identify any gaps in information. Once you've identified the specific pieces of information that you need, schedule an interview with the appropriate person within the organization. For example, if you are tasked with creating a fact sheet that outlines the different types of hotel rooms and suites offered at a luxury resort, you'll want to meet with the person who is most familiar with and knowledgeable on this topic, such as the resort's vice president of hotel operations. Remember, executives are busy. Do them the courtesy of offering to conduct the interview in person, by phone or by email, depending on what best accommodates their schedules.

Following the interview, fill in any remaining gaps in information on the draft. Gather all remaining questions before conducting a follow-up interview (if necessary). Many times, follow-up questions can be accomplished through a quick phone call or email.

Once a draft of the background material has been completed, email the draft to the interviewee for review, edits and any feedback. Incorporate any needed edits into the draft and submit a final version of the draft to the interviewee for approval. Once approved, email the approved draft to your supervisor for any additional edits before finalizing the backgrounder and adding it to your organization's arsenal of public relations materials.

Form

Background materials take many forms, including backgrounders, fact sheets, bio sketches, feature articles, by-line articles and opinion pieces. Like media pitches and advisories/alerts, background materials are not intended for publication. Their primary purpose is to provide members of the media with additional, or background, information on an organization and its people, products, services and initiatives, so that they can properly prepare their stories.

This chapter will specifically examine the background material called a backgrounder.

Backgrounders

As mentioned above, *background materials* include a variety of materials used to provide media members with additional information on a certain topic relating to an organization. A *backgrounder*, on the other hand, is a specific type of background material and should not be confused with the umbrella term background materials.

A backgrounder is an informational piece that is "an expanded version of the history, mission, goals, and purpose of an organization" (Diggs-Brown, 2013, p. 64). Typically written in paragraph form, backgrounders provide more in-depth information about an organization and are generally one page or longer, although they can also be shorter. They often include the organization's history, mission and vision statements, values, organizational policies and a full description of what the organization does.

"Backgrounders should not have a *who, what, where, when, why, how* lead — that's the job of news releases ... Backgrounders are much more like encyclopedia entries than news stories" (Marsh, Guth, & Poovey Short, 2012, p. 78).

Backgrounders can be used in print form (e.g., included a print media kit), digital form (e.g., included in a digital media kit, such as a USB flash drive) or online (e.g., posted to an organization's online press room or even in the "About" or "Bio" sections of an organization's social media channels).

Structure

One of the most commonly used backgrounders is called a *historical backgrounder*, which "gives a chronological account of the history of an organization, the birth and evolution of a product, or the origins of a program or issue" (Zappala & Carden, 2010, p. 136).

Like news releases, backgrounders are written in block paragraph form, in third-person with a factual tone. Unlike news releases, backgrounders do not have newspaper-style headlines; instead, they use simple titles, such as the name of organization or event being described.

When crafting backgrounders, public relations writers need to be mindful of not using language that will date the piece. While some information will need to be updated on a regular basis (e.g., the number of locations a hotel chain has), most information should be written in a way that doesn't date itself. For example, instead of stating, "The organization was founded 10 years ago," simply write, "The organization was founded in 2009." Backgrounders should aspire to be what we call "evergreens" — pieces that are always current and relevant.

Let's examine a basic structure that can be used when writing a historical backgrounder. While backgrounders can also be structured in a Q&A format or broken up with subheads, the suggested structure below is reflective of most backgrounders.

Logo

Although not required, many backgrounders include the organization's logo in the header area.

Title

Most backgrounders include a title in bold. While some are simply titled "Backgrounder," most choose a title that would be better understood by readers and/or includes the organization's name. For example, "About Us," "About The Salvation Army," or "A History of The Salvation Army."

Note: Since backgrounders use titles, not newspaper-style headlines, it is not necessary to use Downstyle (See Chapter 1 for more guidance). Most titles capitalize proper nouns and prepositions with four or more letters. How your organization chooses to format its title is ultimately a style preference.

Body

The body of the backgrounder features block paragraphs detailing the history and mission of the organization in chronological order, beginning with the founding or creation of the organization and traveling to present day.

The first sentence typically introduces the organization and states its mission and the date it was established. For example, "Farmhouse Foods was established in 1985 with the mission of making organic foods and products more accessible and affordable to families in the United States."

The second sentence serves as a transition into chronicling the organization's history: "The company was founded by a group of dairy farmers in Auburn, Alabama, eager to get their organic milk, butter and cheese into local grocery stories and eateries."

The sentences and paragraphs that follow the transition sentence should continue to tell the story chronologically. "Following its quick success partnering with local establishments, the band of farmers set out to expand its network. In 1988, the company added farmers from Birmingham and Atlanta and grew its list of participating farms from 10 to 50."

There is no set, required number of paragraphs for the narrative. When writing backgrounders for organizations that are decades or centuries old, public relations writers may need a page or more in order to fully communicate the organization's rich history while newly established organizations may only require a few paragraphs.

Regardless of length, the backgrounder should conclude by bringing the reader to the present day. For example, "Today, Farmhouse Foods operates a network of more than 500 farms across the country who supply grocery stores, eateries and boutique shops with organic foods and products."

Backgrounder Template

LOGO

Title of Backgrounder
The backgrounder should use block paragraphs to tell the organization's story chronologically. Your first sentence/paragraph should state when the organization was founded along with its purpose and/or mission statement. This may also include the city and state or country where the organization was founded.

Next, a transition sentence is needed to kick off the organization's story from its beginning. See the "Structure" section above for more guidance.

Continue to chronicle the organization's history using block paragraphs until you've reached the present day.

❖ PERSPECTIVE FROM THE PROS

By Merrie Meyers

A backgrounder offers a prime opportunity to positively frame an issue for a client or employer. Unlike a press release, traditionally used to announce something new, the backgrounder allows the creator to bring in historical, political and/or social context into the scenario, providing greater understanding of an issue or event.

Years ago, our local school district received a grant to preserve old Dillard, also known as "the Colored School," the first school built to educate African American children in Fort Lauderdale during the first half of the 20th century.

On its own, a preservation grant award is significant, as most grants don't support capital/building projects. The backgrounder on the award provided the history of the school and what it represented, then and now. The content demonstrated that project partners — the school board, the city of Fort Lauderdale and the Black Historical Society — shared an ongoing commitment to preserving and celebrating the accomplishments of all students: past, present and future.

Without the benefit of the backgrounder, which was packaged as an addendum to the grant award press release, the significance would have been missed by the media — most of whom were not alive when the school was in operation. The backgrounder also provided tangible evidence of the school district's community outreach efforts within the African American community.

Exercise

Exercise 8.1 – Crafting a Backgrounder

Reach out to a local nonprofit or student organization and offer to help the organization build its brand presence by creating a backgrounder for it.

First, conduct secondary research to gather any existing information about the organization (e.g., news articles, fact sheets, organizational charts, website content, etc.).

Next, use the information to develop a draft of a backgrounder that follows the backgrounder template presented in this chapter.

Once you have a draft of the backgrounder, identify any gaps in information to develop interview questions for a member of the organization's leadership team. Schedule and conduct an in-person, phone or email interview with that person to gather the remaining information.

Following the interview, complete the backgrounder draft and submit it to your organization's contact to review for any feedback, including the identification of any factual errors.

Make any requested edits and submit the final backgrounder.

References

Diggs-Brown, B. (2013). *The PR Styleguide: Formats for Public Relations Practice.* Boston, MA: Wadsworth Cengage Learning.

Marsh, C., Guth, D.W., & Poovey Short, B. (2012). *Strategic Writing: Multimedia Writing for Public Relations, Advertising and More.* Upper Saddle River, NJ: Pearson.

Zappala, J.M., & Carden, A.R. (2010). *Public Relations Writing Worktext: A Practical Guide for the Profession* (3rd ed.). New York, NY: Routledge.

Chapter 9

Fact Sheets

Whitney Lehmann

Purpose

In addition to backgrounders, explored in Chapter 8, fact sheets are another type of background material that public relations professionals can use to provide media writers and other publics with additional information.

Fact sheets summarize key facts about an organization or its people, products, services, events or initiatives. They are short documents, typically one page in length, that communicate information in a concise format to give journalists, employees, customers and other publics a general understanding of a subject.

"Fact sheets are designed to inform. They briefly summarize the scope of an organization's services and influences, the features and benefits of a new product, the extent of a problem, or the significance of a social issue" (Zappala & Carden, 2010, p. 133).

Fact sheets take different forms depending on their purpose. A traditional or standard fact sheet communicates fundamental information about an organization, such as its key executives/leadership, its address and/or various locations, its various branches or departments, its products, services or other offerings, and its website, phone number and social media channels, among other pieces of information.

In addition to providing an overview of an organization, standard fact sheets can also be used to communicate information about specific products, brands, services or initiatives within an organization. For example, a cosmetics company preparing to launch a new line of eco-friendly beauty products could develop a fact sheet to highlight the line and its features.

A historical fact sheet is similar to a historical backgrounder in that it chronicles the history of an organization, but it is typically written in bullet form rather than in paragraph form. A historical fact sheet also tends to focus more on highlighting important milestones in a company's history, as opposed to a backgrounder that shares an organization's full story with rich detail.

A special-event fact sheet can be created for one-time or recurring events, such as an annual fundraiser. A special-event fact sheet describes the event and its purpose, provides a brief history of the event (if applicable), and lists participants, sponsors, beneficiaries and event contacts.

Format

While backgrounders are written in paragraph form, traditional fact sheets typically use bulleted or numbered items, although other formats for fact sheets do exist. Other popular formats include:

- Question & Answer (Q&A) series or Frequently Asked Questions (FAQ) about a subject followed by answers written in paragraph form.
- Infographic that can visually explain a product or service in more detail.
- Timeline that chronicles important milestones in an organization's history.
- Organizational chart that illustrates the structure of an organization and the relationships and relative ranks of its parts and positions/jobs.
- Glossaries, which provide definitions of terms/language that may be unfamiliar to journalists or consumers.
- "Points of Pride" that provides a bulleted list of the organization's awards/accomplishments.
- Narrative or news-story form, often with subheads throughout to segment and organize the information (similar to a backgrounder).
- And more!

There is no "correct" format for a fact sheet, as the type of information a public relations writer is attempting to communicate should ultimately dictate the format. For example, if a public relations writer working for an athletic apparel company is tasked with creating a fact sheet to inform customers about the features of its new running shoe, an infographic-type fact sheet illustrating the shoe's different features might work best. Or, let's say, a public relations writer working for a pharmaceutical company is tasked with creating a fact sheet that communicates important information to consumers about a new drug. In this case, a Q&A or FAQ format might be most appropriate.

Regardless of format, the information presented in a fact sheet should be organized in an identifiable order. Standard fact sheets can be organized by topic through subheads. For example, "About Us," "Locations," "Products & Services," etc. Subheads can also be conversational. For instance, "Who Are We?" "What Do We Do?" "Meet Our Team" etc.

Fact sheets presented through a Q&A or FAQ format are also organized using subheads, but in this case, the subheads are questions. For example, "What are the side effects associated with using this drug?"

Narrative or news-story form fact sheets should be structured using an inverted pyramid while historical fact sheets should be organized chronologically through major milestones.

Structure

Header

Like backgrounders, fact sheets do not use headlines; they use basic titles such as "Fact Sheet," "About Us" or a title that is reflective of the subject matter. The header area typically features the organization's logo and/or a logo for a special event.

Body

For traditional fact sheets that use bulleted items, the information can be presented in full sentences or in words or phrases. What's important is that the bulleted items are consistent in their format. Again, the content should dictate whether the fact sheet uses full sentences or simple words or phrases.

For example, a historical fact sheet would be best communicated through full sentences (e.g., "In 2012, the company held its initial public offering (IPO)") versus a fact sheet introducing customers to a new flavored water that would most likely use words or phrases to describe the product's features (e.g., "Zero calories," "Natural flavors," "Sodium-free," etc.).

❖ PERSPECTIVE FROM THE PROS

By Merrie Meyers

Just like the backgrounder referenced in Chapter 8, a fact sheet offers an entity the opportunity to control the information provided about the organization. A fact sheet does contain just the facts, but, *the facts from the perspective of your employer or client*. Traditionally, fact sheets were used either as stand-alone handouts or more likely as part of a media kit. In today's digital world, there are often hyperlinks within the e-media kit and/or a separate page in the press or media relations section of a website.

There is no one way to create a fact sheet. Unlike the days in which fact sheets were rolled out off a typewriter, today's fact sheets are marvels of graphic design and use creative ways to showcase earnings, stock prices, market position, customer segmentation, key metrics, etc.

Regardless of how your fact sheet shapes up, here are some elements traditionally included in a factsheet:

IMPORTANT

Logo. Fact sheets should always be presented using an official logo at the top of the content. If you are creating a fact sheet for an event, organized by a larger enterprise, (for example, the American Cancer Society's Relay for Life), you'll include the event logo and the sponsoring brand/organization logo. In some instances, a broadly commercial event (think sporting event: NASCAR Racing, Super Bowl, All Star Games) may have an official logo at the top and sponsor logos down the sides and/or across the bottom of the content. There is no one way to create a fact sheet. Most importantly, a fact sheet included in an e-media kit/website should have the same look/design as the larger content.

Senior/Executive Leadership. List the people in charge and the key contacts/managers. Again, if this is a sub event for a brand/entity, you'll want to provide a link to the parent company, but keep this information focused on the matter at hand.

Key Products/Key Markets. This is specific to the organization's bottom line. What do they make/sell/do? Where do they do it? You don't have to list everything and everywhere, again links are helpful, but the top products and markets are important. You may also want to share information about shareholders, customer groups, etc.

Founded/Headquarters. This should reflect the individuals or entities that founded the organizations/event, the year that occurred and where the main base of operations is located. An address, phone number, website and if publicly traded, stock symbol, is always helpful. If the company is multi-national, specify whether this is the U.S. Headquarters, International Headquarters, etc. If needed, list both.

Funding/Financing. For-profit corporations typically include earnings, key metrics for their production/sales process. Startups often include information about the venture capital investors/angel investors/GoFundMe resources or foundation support. Non-profit entities may share information about what services are provided through funding. Fund raising events — for example, walkathons — might indicate the amount of funds raised through the enterprise.

USP/Benefits. What are the unique characteristics of the event/organization? This is something that distinguishes your group/organization/event from everyone else in your market niche? Do you only serve young adults with disabilities? Do you offer services in three languages? Has the entity/enterprise received any significant awards (think major recognitions; Pulitzer, Nobel, Medal of Freedom)?

Contact Information. How can we get more information? Make sure to list the official contact and/or hyperlinks for accessing additional information. Remember to include links to additional documents such as annual reports or stock filings, as well as Instagram, Facebook, Twitter, Pinterest and YouTube sites.

Exercise

Exercise 9.1 – Fact Sheet

You are the public relations manager for Farmhouse Foods. The company is preparing to launch its organic flavored-milk line called Holy Cow! that will be sold in grocery stores nationwide beginning this spring. Using the information below, create a fact sheet that communicates information about this product to consumers wanting to know more about the product. As the public relations representative, you decide which fact sheet format best communicates the information.

The Holy Cow! flavored-milk line will be available in select grocery stores and organic markets beginning April 1, 2020, and will be sold in more than 10,000 stores nationwide. The line is USDA certified organic and features low-fat milk in three flavors: chocolate, strawberry and vanilla.

Holy Cow! milks will be available by the half gallon and as 8-ounce single servings that come in a case of eight. An 8-ounce serving is 150 calories, contains 8 grams of protein, and accounts for 20% of the recommended daily value for calcium.

All Holy Cow! milks are free of artificial flavors and colors and contain DHA Omega-3 to support brain and eye health. Other ingredients include: Grade A Low-fat Organic Milk, Organic Cane Sugar, Organic Natural Flavor, Salt, Vitamin A and Vitamin D3.

Farmhouse Foods is America's #1 organic dairy brand. A full list of products can be viewed at www.farmhousefoods.com/products

Learn more about Farmhouse Foods' Holy Cow! line by visiting www.farm-housefoods.com/holycow or following it on Facebook, Twitter and Instagram @holycowmilks

Reference

Zappala, J.M., & Carden, A.R. (2010). *Public Relations Writing Worktext: A Practical Guide for the Profession* (3rd ed.). New York, NY: Routledge.

Chapter 10

Bio Sketches

Whitney Lehmann

Purpose

While backgrounders chronicle the history of an organization, a *biographical sketch*, also known as a *biography* or *bio sketch*, chronicles the career of a specific individual.

Another type of background material, bio sketches provide background information on a person and are developed for founders, officers and other key players within an organization. Similar to backgrounders, bio sketches are used to familiarize members of the media with a specific topic relating to an organization — in this case, its people.

Like other background materials, bio sketches are not intended for publication. They can be included with a pitch, accompany a news release, posted to an online newsroom, or included in a media kit, so that journalists have the information they need when preparing their stories.

For example, let's say you are the public relations representative for a restaurant that's planning its grand opening, and you want to pitch the opening to a producer of a local TV show that features a "Where to Eat this Week" segment. When pitching the story, you'll want to include a news release that includes important details about the opening, the restaurant and its cuisine, as well as bio sketches for the restaurant owner, its head chef, pastry chef and any other key players from the restaurant who might be featured in a story or segment about the opening.

Bio sketches are written in third person and typically include a person's current position, previous positions, education, professional associations, awards and honors, and, if appropriate, personal information, such as city/state of residence and information related to family life and hobbies. They also include a *headshot*, a professional photo of a person's head and face, or a *portrait* shot, which conveys something about the person's personality or tells the person's story.

Public relations professionals are often charged with interviewing executives to develop their bio sketches. Prior to interviewing an executive, PR writers should ask the individual for his or her resume and use that information to draft an outline of the bio sketch. Any remaining gaps in information should become interview questions. Bio sketches should be updated at least once a year.

PR professionals may also be tasked with booking and coordinating photo shoots with professional photographers in order to secure headshots for key members of an organization. The digital files for headshots, including high-resolution and low-resolution options, should be saved and organized with other public relations materials for quick and easy access. Headshots should be updated regularly as needed.

Format and Structure

Bio sketches are written in block-paragraph form and generally include the person's headshot, although professional portrait shots can also be used.

Like a backgrounder, there is no set length for a bio sketch. Bio sketches can be successfully written in one to two paragraphs or, depending on the amount of detail, can include several paragraphs.

Bio sketches typically include the following information in this order:

Bio Sketch Title

Bio sketches are titled with the person's full name, position and the name of the organization. For example:

Lance Samuels, Ph.D.

CEO, Mission Works Inc.

Name: State the person's full name, including any academic, religious, legislative, military and/or royal titles (see the "names" and "titles" entries in the AP Stylebook for more guidance). Note that firefighters and police officers use military-style titles (see the "military titles" entry). Typically, post-nominal letters are reserved for terminal-level degrees, such as M.D., Ph.D. or the highest degree within a particular field; however, non-terminal degrees and professional licenses, may be included as well, depending on the organization's style preference or the person's preference.

When listing multiple sets of post-nominal letters, LinkedIn (2016) suggests this order for professionals in the United States, although this order may vary by country or region:

1. Religious institutes.
2. Theological degrees.
3. Academic degrees.
4. Honorary degrees, honors, decorations.
5. Professional licenses, certifications, affiliations.
6. Retired uniformed service.

For academic degrees, list only the highest degree earned. One exception, however, is when an individual has earned both a doctorate-level degree and an MBA or professional degree. In this case, list them both. For example, "Victoria Barney, Ph.D., MBA."

Per AP Style, do not use courtesy titles, such as Miss, Ms., Mr. or Mrs. Use the name a person prefers (Tom versus Thomas). If a nickname is included with a person's name, put quotation marks around it (Paul "Bear" Bryant). See the AP Style "pseudonyms, nicknames" entry.

Title/Organization: State the person's formal title followed by the name of the organization (e.g., "Director of Business Development, Global Health Co.). See the AP Stylebook entries "company, companies," "company names" and "corporation" for guidance on abbreviations (e.g., Co., Cos., Corp., Inc., etc.). Do not use a comma before Inc. or Ltd., even if one is included in the formal title.

Headshot

The person's headshot typically appears below the person's name and title and before the body of the bio sketch, although bio sketches can be formatted in a number of ways. The decision to use a headshot versus a less formal portrait shot is a style preference and should speak to the industry and organizational culture. For example, while headshots might be more appropriate for bio sketches written for the partners of a law firm, playful portrait shots could be a good fit for bio sketches created for executives of a toy company.

Body

The body of the bio sketch is written in block paragraph form using inverted pyramid style and generally includes the below information in this order:

Current Position: The first paragraph introduces the person's full name, title and job duties.

"James Avery is the vice president of communications for Global Health Co. In this role, he leads the strategic direction of a broad range public relations and marketing activities for the organization and oversees a communications team with more than 50 staff members."

More than one sentence, or paragraph, may be needed to communicate the individual's primary job duties.

Career History: The second block of information segues into the person's career history and details previous positions held at the organization, positions held with other employers and/or relevant work experiences.

"Prior to joining Global Health Co., Avery served as the vice president of marketing and communications for Health Systems Inc. and as the director of media relations for Hope Hospital in Chicago, Illinois."

This paragraph may also include a basic overview of job duties or major accomplishments associated with previous positions.

"During his time as director of media relations for Hope Hospital, national media coverage for the hospital increased by 50%."

Membership/Leadership in Professional Organizations: Once you've detailed the subject's current and previous positions, the next paragraph(s) should communicate additional information about the individual pertaining to his or her career, including membership and leadership positions in professional and trade organizations. This section can also include any service/volunteer work.

"Avery is a member of the Public Relations Society of America (PRSA), the Healthcare Communications Association (HCA) and the Society for Health Communication. He served as the HCA president from 2000 to 2005."

Education/Certifications/Awards & Honors: Following any involvement in professional associations, list any earned degrees, licenses, certifications, accreditations, awards or honors. Degrees should be listed from highest to lowest rank.

"Avery holds a Ph.D. in Communication from Sunshine State University, an M.A. in Public Relations from Bay State University and a B.A. in Communication Studies from Bay State University."

See the AP Style entry "academic degrees" for guidance on writing the names of degrees.

This section should also include any relevant professional licenses, certifications and/or accreditations.

"He earned an Accreditation in Public Relations (APR) in 2010."

Conclude this block of information by listing any significant awards or honors.

"In 2015, Avery was named Communicator of the Year by the Health Communications Association. In 2019, he was elected to the prestigious PRSA College of Fellows, which recognizes the industry's 'best of the best' public relations practitioners."

Personal Information: Depending on the organization's and/or subject's preference, a bio sketch may or may not contain personal information. If personal information is included, it should be the final piece of information included, and it should be brief. City and state of residence, family life and hobbies are popular pieces of personal information included in bio sketches.

"Avery lives in Palo Alto, California, with his wife, son and two rescue dogs. When he's not busy leading the strategic direction for Global Health Co.'s various communication channels, he enjoys spending time with his family, traveling, and participating in 5K runs."

Bio Sketch Template

Person's Full Name
Position/Title, Name of Organization
←INSERT HEADSHOT HERE→

The body of a bio sketch should be written using block paragraphs with single spacing between sentences and double spacing between paragraphs. The first paragraph should introduce the individual with his or her full name and current position and also detail the major duties associated with this position.

The second paragraph typically transitions into the individual's career history and lists previous positions held at the organization or with past employers. This section may also include duties or accomplishments associated with previous positions.

Once current and previous positions have been explained, detail any membership and/or leadership positions the subject has associated with professional and trade organizations. This section may also include service or volunteer work.

After describing any activity with professional organizations, detail the individual's education, including any degrees/licenses earned, certifications and/or accreditations. This section should also include any significant awards or honors.

A final, optional paragraph can include personal information about the individual, such as city/state of residence, family life and hobbies.

❖ PERSPECTIVE FROM THE PROS

By Merrie Meyers

A bio sketch is a brief overview of an individual that is somewhere between a resume and a biography. The optimal word in that sentence is **brief**. Writing a good bio sketch is both an art and a science. It requires highly developed writing and editing skills. In one to two paragraphs, you need to sum up the essence of the 5 W's and the H. It should provide an effective and honest reflection of yourself, presenting your personal brand to create a good first impression.

The bio sketch should offer the reader specific details about you and your accomplishments. If you've ever read a book jacket, you've read a bio sketch. All we need to know is a little background about the individual to help us understand the context of their involvement with the project, event or publication, etc.

A bio sketch provides a brief introduction of a speaker to an audience, just enough to help them understand the reason for your involvement in an occasion or perhaps the importance of your connection to an event. This can range from introduction of the best man at a wedding to the presentation of a speaker at an awards ceremony or a TED Talk.

It is typical to be asked to write your own bio sketch. After all, who knows you best? This may be one of the hardest writing assignments you've ever tackled. How do you get your essence down to a couple of sentences?

Here are some ideas that will help you create a bio sketch:
- Assume that the reader or listener doesn't know you. Provide your name, training (degrees if relevant) and recent accomplishments.
- Write in third person since this is likely to be read by someone else about or for you.
- Keep it current. Bio sketches should be updated frequently as situations and accomplishments, change.
- Know/learn about the audience. If the audience will appreciate it, humor can help establish your brand. Depending on the purpose of the event, spouses, partners, kids and critters could be referenced in a bio sketch.

Exercises

Exercise 10.1 – Bio Sketch

Using the bio sketch structure and template from this chapter, write a bio sketch for yourself in one to two paragraphs. Students should list their degree program as their current position. For example: "Emily Duncan is a communication major in the B.A. in Communication program at Nova Southeastern University. As a communication major, Duncan XYZ ..."

Exercise 10.2 – AP Style Skill Drill

Locate 10 errors in the bio sketch below related to Associated Press Style. Use AP Style Editing Symbols to correct the errors.

Dr. Stephanie Ramirez is a Professor of Writing in the Sunshine State University Department of Writing. In this role, she teaches a variety of undergraduate courses for the university's Bachelor of Arts in Professional Writing program and serves as the Executive Director for the Sunshine State Writing and Communication Center.

Ramirez holds a Ph.D. in Writing and Rhetoric from Syracuse University, a MA in English and American Literature from Boston College, & a BA in English from New York University.

Reference

Vildibill, W. (January 15, 2016). Etiquette for the alphabet soup of post-nominal letters. Retrieved from www.linkedin.com/pulse/ etiquette-alphabet-soup-post-nominal-letters-will-vildibill-mba-pmp

Chapter 11

News Writing

Heidi Carr

I'll let you in on a secret.

I've spent days with a blank screen in front of me, wondering how on earth to tell the tale of the news story.

It's not writer's block. It's just the challenge of "how to start."

So, I decided to do what I would do with any regular news story. I just skipped the lede and began putting later parts of the chapter down on paper, knowing I could always come back and think of the first paragraph or even rewrite the piece.

And that is exactly how you write a news story.

Understanding What's Newsworthy

First, let's consider, what is a news story and what makes it different from a feature story?

A news story should contain information that is just coming to light. It can be under the umbrella of dozens of topics: Crime, politics, disasters, policy changes, education, finances, breaking news in the entertainment industry, transportation, science, medical … you get the idea.

It can educate, it can inform, and it can entertain.

A feature story may be a story that is entertaining, may be educational and has a bit of a shelf life. It doesn't contain any urgent material. Examples might be a profile on a celebrity, or a piece on traveling to Bora Bora.

And then there's the hybrid, a news-feature. This is sometimes called a sidebar. It's a colorful story that has some news elements.

For example, let's say the Chicago Cubs are playing in the World Series. In addition to covering the actual games, other stories that might be done include:

Breaking news: One of the star players is injured in a boating accident on Lake Michigan the weekend before a game. He suffered a broken clavicle and won't be able to play for the rest of the season. The operator of the other boat was charged with DUI.

Feature: Meet the 10-year-old mega fan who takes off his shirt at the games, mugs for the TV cameras and flexes his muscles. He's there at every game with his grandpa and even has a little dance. The players consider him a good luck charm.

News Feature: Cubbies fans are flocking from all over the country to root on their team. This is a big boom for the travel industry. Hotels are booked solid; there are lines out the door at sports bars and tours of the stadium on "off days" are sold out. It's bringing in millions of extra tourism dollars to the city.

Is it Worth a Story?

When someone approaches you with a tip for a story idea, here are some questions to ask yourself:

- Do you find it interesting?
- Is it something other people will find interesting?
- Will it have impact on people's lives? The environment? Public policy? The pocketbook? Will people talk about it?
- When did it happen? If it's something that happened a while back, it may have lost its news value. An event that has just recently happened or is about to happen has more news value.
- Does a story "have legs"? This means that there has been news reported, but more news is coming out of it. Take the above example of the poor player in the boating accident. This isn't a one-cycle news story. There will be "folos" on that — who were the people on the boats? What was the extent of their injuries? What is happening to the driver charged with DUI? Is he in jail? Who is replacing the star player on the field? Are his injuries improving?

Accuracy Trumps Everything

There's a famous phrase in journalism schools: "If your mother says she loves you, check it out."

In other words, never take anything at face value.

Check the facts your sources tell you. You have to go to the original source — whether it's the doctor who is performing the never-before-done surgery, the police department who responded, the hero who jumped in the lake and saved people's lives, the victims of the accident — and interview them yourself. You need to check records. You need to talk to multiple sources.

Never assume that what someone tells you is true. They may intentionally be trying to mislead you, or they just have made an innocent error. The bottom line is the viewer or reader doesn't know where the inaccurate information came from. They just know you are the one reporting it.

If you end up writing something that contains a factual error, you will lose all credibility. And once lost, it's impossible to get it back.

Even what may come across to you as a small error, such as a math error or spelling a person's name wrong, will put doubt in the audience's mind. If they know that you have gotten a figure wrong, how can they trust anything else you've included in your story.

Go back and redo the math, triple check the spelling of the names, and never make an assumption.

Remember this adage: Assume = Making an ass out of u and me.

The Elements of a News Story

- lede
- nut graf
- quotes
- anecdote/examples/facts
- explanatory — why should we care? What does it mean?
- what's next?
- the kicker

The Lede

I bet you are noticing the spelling. It's not wrong. The way you start a news or feature story is called a lede by journalists.

Your goal is to write something that gives an idea of what the story is about, do it in a way that grabs the audience's attention, and keep it concise.

It ain't easy.

As I mentioned above in my lede, sometimes it helps if you just write "LEDE GOES HERE" and then start writing what you have. You can always delete, move things around or simply rewrite.

Two Types of Ledes
- Straight lede — just goes into the who, what, when, where, why and how.
- Anecdotal lede — paints a scene with a few details, which can help the reader feel there in person.

The Dos and Don'ts of Writing Ledes
- Do make sure your lede gives an idea of what the following paragraphs are about. If your lede can go on top of *any* story, then it's not good enough.
- Don't start your story with the opposite of what your story is about.
- "On a typical Saturday morning, Sam sleeps in till noon. But this morning, she jumped out of bed at 5 a.m., put on her running shoes, and took the first steps into what will be her future — training for a marathon."
- If it's not relevant to the story, you don't want to start out with it.
- Avoid starting a story with a quote. I know you want to. Resist.

Example

Right: A sexism row has engulfed the new British prime minister after he suggested women only attend university in order to find a husband. Boris Johnson jokingly commented that women are going to college because they "had to find men to marry."

Wrong: "Female students are going to universities because they have got to find men to marry," British Prime Minister Boris Johnson jokingly said in response to a comment that 68% of the women in Malaysia would go to college.

● Don't start your story with the day of the week. Make that first word really important. The day can be in the first sentence, but does it warrant being the first word your audience reads or hears?

Example

Right: Gold prices breached the $1,500 per ounce level on Wednesday for the first time in more than 11 years, signaling precious metals are again becoming a place for investors to store their assets as the stock market continues to wobble.

Wrong: On Wednesday, gold prices breached the $1,500 per ounce level for the first time in more than 11 years ...

● Do keep your lede as simple to read as possible. Avoid putting names and titles in the first sentence unless they are already well known. It's better to use something that describes the person rather than their name.

Would you find it more interesting to read a story that began "Karen Black was the winner of Friday's Baltimore Marathon," or "A new mother who gave birth three weeks ago was the winner of Friday's Baltimore Marathon. Karen Black, whose daughter Natalie cheered her mother from the sidelines in the arms of her father, crossed the finish line a full 2 minutes ahead of her closest competitor."

Nut Graf

This usually comes after the lede. It may be the second paragraph or it may be a little lower, but it should be very high up in your story. The purpose of the nut graf is to get across the gist of the story. It should contain the who, what, when, where, why and how if they haven't been covered in the lede.

Quotes

Try to get a voice up high in your story. Let us hear from someone involved, whether it's a politician or a participant.

Your quote should be on the same topic as the lede and nut graf.

Story Organization

How should your story unfold?

It could be chronologically, or it could be ping-ponging opinions on particular points, or it could be by topic.

For example, if you are telling the story of our new mom marathon winner, you could organize the story chronologically, which would include her training, being pregnant and having the baby, deciding after the birth whether she was ready to compete, the day of the race and her family being there.

If you tell it from different viewpoints, you could get Black's decision to run just after giving birth and then bring her doctor's opinion, and perhaps the sentiments of the marathon organizers, her trainer and other runners.

If you decide to do it by similar topics, you might follow up your lede and quote with Black getting back into shape after giving birth, and then go back to her history as a marathon runner, and then working in her doctor's guidance.

Anecdote/Example/Facts

There's a saying — don't tell me, show me. What this means is don't just write "Black trained hard." Give specifics. At what hour did she get up in the morning? Did she train on a track or on a treadmill, what exercises did she do, how many miles did she start at doing, how did she balance working out and taking care of a newborn? How many hours of sleep did she get? What foods did she eat? What specific advice did her coach give her? The more precise you are with these details, the better your story will be.

Explanatory

Usually, at some point in your story, you need to zoom out and give the big picture. Each story is a microcosm. In the case of Karen Black, is our marathon mom an example of a trend? Are female athletes jumping back into their sport quickly after giving birth? Are doctors encouraging this? What effects can this have on their bodies and breastfeeding?

What's Next?

If possible, spin your story forward. Don't let it end in the present. Where is this likely to lead? What could happen? What's expected to happen? Take the reader into the future.

The Kicker

You may have heard of the "inverted pyramid" style of writing, where you start with the most important information and as you go further into the story, the information becomes less interesting, necessary or relevant.

That's the old way of doing it. It was necessary when news stories were cut on the composing room floor — the editor would just use a razor blade to trim the story from the bottom.

But with desktop publishing, it is much easier for an editor and designer to make the story fit the space or time.

And that's why it's more important today to make your ending — or kicker — really count. You want people to read to the end, and when it's the end, know it.

Hint: a quote often makes for the perfect ending.

Do not end a news story with a paragraph summarizing the information in the story, or your own opinion on the news.

Writing and Rewriting

You will rarely submit the very first thing you write.

As your facts come in, get them on the screen in front of you. As you begin writing, one sentence will flow into another and very quickly, you'll have ... something to rewrite.

Make sure you include all the pertinent information — who, what, when, where, why and how.

Now step away and remember that you are an "expert" on the topic, but your reader is coming in not knowing anything. So you need to make sure what you write is understandable to someone just learning about it for the first time.

Keep it to one point per paragraph. Every time you bring up a new point, or start a quote, create a new paragraph. Keep numbers to a minimum. Simplify complicated information. Give a little background — but don't start out with the background.

When you have compelling facts, strong anecdotes and winning quotes, you don't need to "overwrite" the story. Just let these elements tell the story. The simpler your writing is, the better your story will read.

Step away from your work and then come back and read it. Does it flow from one point to the other? Is there anything that sounds like jargon? Do you have anecdotes and quotes to illustrate the points you want to make.

Scan for any adverbs (words that end with "ly"). Take them out.

Now look at the verbs. Are they strong verbs? Can you find a verb that's even more precise?

Example:

Which of these sentences do you like best?

A)   The cat walked carefully along the kitchen countertop.
B)   The cat tiptoed on the kitchen countertop.

Tiptoed is much more precise than walked carefully — and it's half the syllables.

What other verbs are more descriptive than "walked"?

Sauntered, strutted, paced, patrolled, pranced, traipsed and treaded each create a vision.

The Thesaurus is your friend (just don't turn into Joey Tribbiani on "Friends," who turned, "They're warm, nice people with big hearts" to "They're humid, prepossessing Homo sapiens with full-sized aortic pumps."

Now Back to That Lede

You've gathered your information. You've got your nut graf, giving a simple explanation of what the story is about. Now it's time to write (or rewrite) that lede sentence to make it grab the reader's attention.

Let's take an example and work through it together.

Here are the facts behind the ordeal of one woman, whose car was knocked off the road by a hit-and-run driver.

The woman, whose name is Tillie Tooter (I am not making this up), was 83 at the time of the accident. She had been on the way to pick up her granddaughter from the airport at 3 a.m. on a Saturday in August when her car was knocked off a major highway in Fort Lauderdale. No one else was on the road at the time to witness the accident.

Tooter's family contacted the police when she didn't show up at the airport, but there were miles to search, and no one had a clue as to what had happened. Tooter had simply vanished.

Three days later, a teenager and his father were picking up trash along the highway when the 15-year-old spotted a car half-buried by foliage, about a 50-foot drop from the bridge. A pair of feet were dangling outside the open car door.

The father called 911, and within minutes, a team of 25 Fire-Rescue personnel was on hand to saw down the trees, chop off the car's roof, and extract Tooter from the car. Exactly 61 minutes after she had been spotted, the octogenarian was put into a basket and lifted onto the highway by a crane. She had spent 78 hours trapped in her car, without food or a bottle of water.

We'll stop here for now. Of all the facts you've been given, summarize what you think the point of your story is.

Is it?:

A. At 3 a.m. on a Saturday, a woman was hit on the highway and the other car drove off.

B. A teenager picking up litter three days later spotted a car in the ravine, which led to the rescue of a woman who'd been missing for more than three days.

C. An 83-year-old woman survived a 50-foot drop from a highway after being rear-ended and spent three days trapped in her car, enduring humid 90-degree temperatures, and no food or water, before a dramatic rescue that included her being lifted out of a ravine by a crane.

While the first two options are definitely interesting and newsworthy, the third option is really what we're talking about.

With just the little information you've gotten from above, you could easily write a short compelling story.

Let's continue gathering facts.

While Tooter is being treated at the hospital hours after the rescue, reporters swarm to hear her tale of survival.

"Be gentle guys," her granddaughter told the media.

But Tooter was more upset by all the insect bites on her skin and the bruises on her face than she was the camera lights and barrage of questions.

She started recalling details of her ordeal.

After getting hit, she remembered her car somersaulting several times as it dropped off the bridge and landed in the trees below. She was caught in the space between the door and the seat, her seatbelt holding her in place.

"I had to release the seat belt because I was lying on my side and the space was narrow, and I'm not that thin," the grandmother said.

When the sun came up the next day and Tooter hadn't seen any signs of a search and rescue team, she knew it was up to her to do something if she was going to survive.

She jabbed the car horn with her foot, hoping someone would hear. She looked for her cellphone, but it had been ejected from the car during the fall.

To pass the time, she sang Big Band hits. When it rained, she used a metallic steering wheel cover to capture the water. She found a cough drop, licked it, then saved the rest for later. She used a sock to sponge up rainwater and sucked it. She popped a button in her mouth and sucked on that to produce saliva.

After nearly three days in the car, she found a grocery store receipt and wrote a farewell note to her family.

Just a few hours later, she saw the teen's face peering down at her.

"Don't go away," she pleaded weakly. She wiggled her feet, hoping he'd spot the movement.

He couldn't hear her, but he saw her feet.

Within minutes, the rescuers arrived.

As the crane began lifting Tooter up to bridge level, she called out to one of her rescuers, "Can you please get my pocketbook?"

The trooper grabbed her stained purse and brought it to the hospital.

"It's a miracle that I am here, because I didn't expect to be," Tooter said.

When Tooter was done with her story, the journalists burst into applause.

So Let's Stop Here

Has the angle of your story changed? It's still a news story, although now you have a lot more details. In addition to Tooter's first-hand experience, there are interviews with her doctors, Fire-Rescue teams and her 15-year-old rescuer.

Would you change your lede?

If we were writing a straight lede for this story, it might go something like this:

An 83-year-old Fort Lauderdale woman trapped three days in her car survived on rainwater and a cough drop until being discovered by a teen picking up litter on the highway.

It's got all the elements — it tells the who, what, when, where and how. It's factual and concise. Nothing wrong with it.

But once you start collecting all the delicious details from her hospital press conference, you've got a news story that is rich with quotes, color, examples and responses. All of these will help the reader feel as though they are in the car with Tooter, watching the delicate rescue, or in the hospital recovery room.

Here's the anecdotal lede that ran in *The Miami Herald* the morning after her rescue (Herald Archives, 2009, para. 1–5):

> As she lay in her mangled car, far beneath the freeway where she had plunged over the guardrail early Saturday morning, Tillie Tooter screamed for help.
>
> For the next three days, the 83-year-old retiree struggled to survive as the temperatures soared to above 90 degrees. She sipped feebly at rainwater caught in a steering-wheel cover while ants and mosquitoes stung her.
>
> Tooter's ordeal ended Tuesday morning when a passerby on the highway spotted her car half-buried in the foliage below. Alive but weak, she was rushed to Broward General Medical Center in Fort Lauderdale, where she was upgraded from critical to serious condition late Tuesday.
>
> "She didn't think she was ever going to see us again," said a relieved Lori Simms, Tooter's granddaughter. "She just wanted hugs and kisses—and water."

This lede sprinkles in the Who, What, When, Where, Why and How like breadcrumbs leading the reader through the story.

Which lede do you like better?

A Happy Ending

And for those of you who are now Googling Tillie Tooter, the story gets better and better. The man who hit Tooter's car came forward, confessed and apologized. He said he fell asleep at the wheel. Tooter forgave him.

Tooter was invited to tell her story on The Rosie O'Donnell show and got a new car (though she never drove along the highway where her accident happened.)

She lived life to the fullest, passing away of natural causes 15 years after the accident, at the age of 98.

Exercise

Exercise 11.1 – News Story

Work with a student organization or a local nonprofit to identify a timely news item (e.g., grant award, upcoming event/fundraiser, new hire, etc.) that you can write about. Using the interview tips provided in Chapter 7, schedule and conduct an interview with a contact from the organization who can provide you with background information about the news item.

Once you've transcribed your interview, use the news story elements outlined in this chapter to craft a news story. Make sure to incorporate AP Style and use a headline in Downstyle (See Chapter 1 for more guidance).

Reference

Herald Archives, M. (2019, July 29). How 83-year-old Tillie Tooter survived 3 days trapped in her car. It involved a button. *Miami Herald, The (FL)*. Available from NewsBank: Access World News: https://infoweb-newsbank-com.ezproxylocal. library.nova.edu/apps/news/document-view?p=AWNB&docref=news/ 174FD2141ED4A788.

Chapter 12

Feature Writing

Michael Laderman

There used to be a saying back when I was a reporter that had to do with sports writers and news writers.

It went: Give a sports writer a news story, and they'll turn it into an award-winning feature piece. But give a news writer a sports story to pen, and they'll turn it into the most boring game recap you ever read in your life.

I never used to believe that back when I was a young reporter, because, I thought, if you knew how to write one way, you could pretty much write any other way. But the truth of the matter is, after 30-plus years of professional experience that is just not the case.

In my experience, I have seen and worked alongside some of the greatest columnists and witnessed their abilities to write whatever kind of article they needed to write. And I had the pleasure of sharing the same pages as some of the very best.

Those columnists can be counted on in crisis, news time, crunch time, deadline time — you name it — to write any kind of story they needed to. What they knew how to do more than anything, though, was tell a story and share their opinion in the most feature way possible.

News writers, I have found, typically cannot put those same types of thoughts into their writings.

Not that I haven't seen any, but rather I have not seen many who have bothered to learn the nuances that need to be within your head, your mind, your body, your heart and your soul when changing your writing style and turning it into that of a feature writer and reporter.

Fast forward to my career within public relations, communications, marketing, advertising and brand management, and the abilities I learned to be able to write feature stories has been a godsend.

Because it is that ability to know when to write a feature and when to be "featurey," with an understanding of not being overly fluffy and as I would call it, "foo-fooey," is a skill that will serve you tremendously well in this career of yours that you are now in.

I must wholeheartedly admit, though, that neither I, nor anyone else has the magic wand to be able to turn a news writer into a feature writer. Neither I, nor anyone else has the magic wand that can suddenly turn your writing style from simplistic to feature.

It literally has to be within you.

Now, here's the key on that phrase. You're not born with it. You don't just have it or don't have it.

I am a proponent of the following statement, which is: You can teach yourself to be any kind of writer, and any kind of publicist, and any kind of communications expert, but you just need to be willing to adapt and to do it.

You need to be willing to not overthink your writing style.

You need to understand and comprehend that feature writing isn't about coming up with as many different words that all say the same thing, but just in a fluffy way.

Feature writing is not just about going into the thesaurus and saying things like "this was excellent, fantastic, superb, tremendous, oh my goodness, we have never seen such tremendous, stupendous, incredible-istic things going on in the world," etc.

Quite frankly, feature writing is the ability to tell a story from the heart.

That's your pullout quote right there: Telling a story from the heart.

It's understanding that, whereas you now have mastered the news cycle, that is mostly about the who, the what, the when, the why, the where, and the how. The feature writing will do all of that. The feature writing will say all of that. But it will expound and expand on all of those nuances.

The feature writing will say not just "the 2019 Clermont Caribbean Jerk Festival will take place this Friday, Saturday or Sunday." What it *will* do is it will tell the story; it will be written as though you are the feature reporter wanting to not just tell the facts but give the story behind it.

As a news writer, you need to do your research to come up with all the proper and appropriate news items that must be contained in that respective article, or in that press release, or in that pitch, or in that calendar announcement, or in that public service announcement.

When you are turning something into a feature, don't just think of the extra special words that you need to tie in to add a couple of extra paragraphs, because that tends to be the thing that most writers who are not comfortable writing this style, do.

They tend to think that feature writing is simply more a chore and a task of coming up with extra paragraphs that just happen to say the same thing over and over, but just in a different way.

And that couldn't be further from the truth.

Writing features, whether as stories or as press releases, is a few small things that make up one big thing on how to do it.

The small things include: Thinking of how you would want to be told the story; thinking of the kind of stories that you enjoy reading; thinking of how when you pick up a story, you don't even know you're reading something because it flows so well; thinking of how, when you pick something up that is clearly a sales pitch with too many of the same words just said differently, you yourself, don't buy into it. You don't believe it; you don't want to read it any more than you already have to at that very point in time.

It's coming up with a story and understanding that you need to write a story that is creative but not overly creative. That it is not fluff. It's just something that expands and expounds upon not just the main facts, but the nuances of the facts that help set up the facts, that help set up the story, that help share and tell the story.

You can always take any feature story and turn it into a news story. But you cannot take a finished news story and truly turn it into a feature story. To write a proper feature is not just about coming up with fluff words. It's about actually understanding the nuances of what it is you are about to write about.

This press release written for the Caribbean American association of Lake County's Clermont Caribbean Jerk Festival was done as a feature purposefully so because, number one, I knew that media outlets in the Central Florida area were interested in running whatever was sent to them. Number two, it was used as a social media post. Number three, it was used on their website.

❖ LAKE COUNTY CARIBBEAN ASSOCIATION HOPES FOR SUNNY SKIES FOR ITS ANNUAL JERK FESTIVAL ON MAY 4TH

CLERMONT, Florida – It has technically been less than a year since 10 consecutive days' of rain flooded the Lake County and overall Central Florida region, but to Stuart Wilson, the memories of that day are as clear as though it were yesterday.

"The skies opened, and they didn't close for a very long time," recalled Wilson, a retired Colonel in the U.S. Air Force who, as a community activist and local photographer, resides in his adopted hometown of Clermont. "While we needed those rains back then, they also put a damper on the community events, which hurt attendance, which hurt fund-raising efforts."

Wilson knows first-hand more than anybody. As president of the Caribbean American Association of Lake County [CAALC], he was a driving force of the non-profit organization's Clermont Caribbean Jerk Festival, its annual event that raises scholarship dollars for graduating high school seniors looking to attend college, university or trade school.

But because of last year's tremendous rains, attendance numbers dropped significantly as the downpour increased. And due to that, CAALC lost thousands of dollars that were to go directly to those student scholarships.

"That is what makes this year's Jerk Festival so important for us," he said, referring to the upcoming eighth annual Clermont Caribbean Jerk Festival, held at Clermont's Waterfront Park on Saturday, May 4th [12 noon – 10 p.m.]. "We are hoping for bright, clear skies this year, so our community can come together again to not only help support our local kids, helping them to continue their education, but also to have a truly fun time with some fantastic Caribbean food and entertainment."

The popular annual Clermont food and music festival has been bringing the Caribbean to Central Florida every summer for the past seven years. This year's festival features the music of FAB 5, the most popular band in the Caribbean, along with the popular Guyanese star Terry Gajraj, and a Jamaican-born favorite Tory Wynter. There will also be activities for children, and plenty of Caribbean food and beverages for kids and adults.

"Their reggae and soca performances have dancers and partygoers all over the Caribbean dancing and partying well into the night," said Wilson, about Fab 5 headlining this year's event. "Their versatility and musical skills enable them to entertain crowds with R&B, funk, gospel, jazz, and disco."

"It will definitely be a fun day and night," added Mitchell Hill, the Festival's new chairman on behalf of CAALC. "We are looking forward to presenting a taste of the Caribbean to all our fellow Central Florida residents. Hopefully we will be blessed with good weather this year, so we can, more importantly, raise scholarship dollars for the kids of our community."

The Caribbean American Association of Lake County takes education seriously by actively serving the young people in our community by providing scholarships and mentoring while developing its cultural diversity. For more information, or to purchase advance tickets to this year's Clermont Caribbean Jerk Festival held on May 4th at Clermont's Waterfront Park, phone 352-978-0813, email CAALC@live.com, or visit www.CAALC-FL.org.

News release courtesy of 20 A-M COMMUNICATIONS

So, due to those multiple uses, this is why that one specific release was written the way it was.

Granted, we still did a more traditional news release. We still wrote the basic information. But all that was still included in our feature release. All of that was still included in our feature story.

It ended up getting picked up by local publications and got a very good play on the social websites.

But can you see the difference? Can you see and understand what we talk about when saying you're not leaving any information out of the feature.

But you're getting more in depth about the nuances and special things about the event and the product and the client.

An issue that too many straight news individuals have is the overthinking. I would see this far too many times. Too many fancy words, all saying the same thing.

I would see this far too many times.

❖ 2019 ELECTED CHAIR OF CLERMONT'S 8TH ANNUAL CARIBBEAN JERK FESTIVAL – MITCHELL HILL

CLERMONT, FL – MAY 4, 2019 – In eager [eager? How do you know?] preparation for the exciting [how do you know it'll be exciting?] 8th Annual Caribbean Jerk Festival the Caribbean American Association of Lake County has elected Mitchell Hill as the 2019 Chairman.

Stuart Wilson stated, "We are thrilled to offer the seat to Mitchell Hill, as we believe he has much to offer with his vast cultural experience and leadership skills. He has the will and motivation to enhance all aspects of the Caribbean Jerk Festival."

Hill's notable achievements exemplify the cultural intelligence and awareness he possesses [editorializing someone's intelligence; unnecessary]. Achievements which include Junior Chamber International (JCI) Senator, first West Indies National to be elected President of ASAC (Association of JCI Senators of the Americas and Caribbean) including Spanish, French, Dutch and English-Speaking Countries within the Americas and past Chairman – Antigua Jaycees Caribbean Queen Show.

"I am honored and thrilled to be the elected Chairman of this year's Jerk Festival," Mitchell Hill claimed. "Going forward, I am eager to be apart of the impact that the festival offers and ready to make our 8th Annual Caribbean Jerk Festival the best one yet, along with the help from all of our dedicated volunteers."

With a new Chairman elected, preparations for the 8th Annual Caribbean Jerk Festival are in full force [are they in full force, or are they just underway?] by an excited [how do you know?] group of volunteers. Very big plans [or are they just plans?] are arising each and every day [that's a far-reaching comment] with the goal of drawing in the crowds to support fundraising for CAALC's scholarship program that supports sending young adults to vocational, technical, and community colleges as well as universities.

ABOUT CARIBBEAN AMERICAN ASSOCIATION OF LAKE COUNTY

The Caribbean American Association of Lake County is a 501(c)3 nonprofit organization focused on giving back to the community and enhancing the lives of the young people in our community. CAALC offers Grants and Scholarships to young community residents, is involved in many Community and Charitable Projects, and host many community events. With over 100 active members, CAALC is an extremely generous force [who says they are extremely generous?] within the community pushing to better the futures of young adults. Located at 614 E Hwy 50 #251 Clermont, FL 34712. Follow us on Facebook @CAALC123 to stay up-to-date on all event information.

News release courtesy of 20 A-M COMMUNICATIONS

Watch yourself doing that. When you are writing a feature, don't allow yourself to do that. Don't allow yourself to get caught up in what a thesaurus tells you to write.

Don't just think of another way to say the same word over and over again.

Come up with a different nuance. Come up with an angle. Because the angle is what makes feature writing strong, different and unique.

Without the angle, it's nothing. It is just a news release with a heck of a lot of synonyms. It's a press release with a heck of a lot of fancy words from a thesaurus.

Whether you're a reporter who is charged with writing a 30-inch story, or if you are that communications expert that understands you need something beyond just a factual story to go on a website or in a community publication, you've got to know what to do.

It's all about engagement. Because the straight fact story is fine to do just what it does. But it doesn't necessarily interest the reader or the viewer.

So now put yourself in the position of the communicator who needs to write not only a straight news piece for the event you are promoting — because many media outlets want it that way — but you've also just received a request for something more featurey.

Come up with something … but don't be afraid of it.

Embrace the challenge to be more creative with your writing, not by adding more fancy words that all same the same thing, but by telling more of a back story to your who, what, when, where, why and how.

And above all, write from the heart.

❖ PERSPECTIVE FROM THE PROS

By Megan Fitzgerald

Whether you're writing news or features, the audience should be central to your story finding and storytelling. The best stories speak to and for the audience they serve.

I remember when I started my internship with the weekend/lifestyle section of the Utica-Observer Dispatch. I was so excited for my first opportunity at entertainment writing. Oh, the fabulous places I would go and the celebrities I would see. Then came my first assignment. I was asked to cover the local ice festival. I'm from Miami, Florida. Not only was this not glamorous, it sounded very cold.

Then came my second story and my first celebrity interview — with Big Bird. Yes, Big Bird. Sesame Street Live was coming to town, and Big Bird and I had a phone interview scheduled.

While the ice festival wasn't the Oscars and Big Bird was no George Clooney, I learned an important lesson. While writing had always been my passion, as a professional writer, I would not always cover things I'm passionate about. As a professional writer, it's about the audience. The community that you serve.

Even if ice festivals don't heat you up, you can still cover them and cover them well. And, while Big Bird may not be high on your list of celebrity interviews, it doesn't mean he has nothing to say. It's our job as writers to think about our audience, so that we can make sure that the stories that matter to them get told and that their voices, big and small, get heard.

Exercise

Exercise 12.1 – Feature Story

Help someone choose a specific story of their life — and write about it.
Minimum: 750 words

Find a friend, classmate or relative. Sit down with them and, using both a notepad and a voice recording app, have a conversation with them. Just start talking with them, and in conversation, pull out an interesting tidbit of their life — and focus on that one specific tidbit for your feature story.

Tell them to delve more in-depth into that specific "topic of interest." And then write a feature story about it.

Tips: Do not go into your interview with a set list of questions to ask. You should only need one initial question to get a conversation such as this going. For example, "Tell me about your life, your experiences that you've lived."

Writing for Digital Media

Chapter 13

Email and Writing for the Web

Whitney Lehmann and Michael North

Email

Purpose

Public relations professionals today use many different communications channels to engage with an organization's publics: print materials, such as an alumni magazine or a media kit passed out to journalists at an event; digital materials, like easy-to-access and downloadable news releases, fact sheets and images posted to an organization's online press room; phone calls, like a quick call to an editor or producer to pitch a story; text messages, such as a text-to-give campaign; social media messages, such as posts to a company's Facebook page or a video apology from a CEO posted to its YouTube channel; and much, much more.

Of all the communications channels that public relations professionals work with on a daily basis, email is perhaps the most utilized channel. Whether we're crafting a media pitch, soliciting potential donors, sharing important updates with people within our organizations, coordinating interviews, disseminating news releases to the media, checking in with vendors for an event, engaging in crisis communications, or tackling any other PR-related activity, we're most likely using email to communicate with our publics.

"Most public relations professionals use email extensively for all aspects of their work. Some receive and send hundreds of email messages each day. Email systems allow a person to send the same message, and attachments, to one, ten or even thousands of people" (Newsom & Haynes, 2014, p. 223).

The above examples illustrate how public relations professionals use email messages countless times a day to communicate a wide variety of information with an organization's internal and external publics.

> The benefits of instantaneous communication unbounded by distance are obvious to public relations and marketing practitioners. Organizations use email as the platform for preparing and disseminating newsletters, fundraising appeals, and news releases for notifying journalists, donors, and other key publics of new information posted as organizational blogs or websites.
>
> (Smith, 2017, p. 283)

Structure

While email messages are used to accomplish a multitude of public relations tasks, all email messages can follow a set structure to organize — and best communicate — the information in them. Let's examine the "anatomy" of an email message and how to be strategic with its various parts.

Header: The header area of an email message contains the follows components:

- **From:** The "From" category contains the name/email address of the sender. The sender can be an individual or a mailbox representing an organization or a department within an organization. For example, "Department of Writing and Communication."
- **To:** The "To" category contains the email addresses for any individual recipients or groups of recipients with whom you are directly communicating with (e.g., "Hi Susan" or "Greetings Parents"). Groups of recipients can be formalized with a distribution list, such as a distribution list for all employees within an organization. Note: Recipients in the "To" line are visible to each other and any other recipients on the email.
- **CC:** "CC" stands for "Carbon Copy." Put recipients here if you want them copied on an email as "for your information" but do not need a response or action from them. Note: Recipients in CC line are visible to all recipients on the email.
- **BCC:** "BCC" stands for "Blind Carbon Copy." Put recipients here if you want them copied on an email to someone else as a "for your information," but you'd like to do so blindly. Recipients in the BCC line are *not* visible to other recipients on the email.
- **Subject:** The subject line for an email should be clear, concise, to-the-point and relevant to the subject matter. It can be written as a phrase (e.g., "HR policy updates," "Sponsorship opportunity" or "Meeting to discuss performance review") or in headline style (e.g., "University to conduct test of emergency notification system") depending on what's most appropriate for and relevant to the recipients you're communicating with. For example, headline-style subject lines that can quickly communicate a news hook might be most effective when emailing members of the media who receive hundreds of emails a day.

Body of Email: The body of an email is structured similarly to a media pitch (Chapter 3), with a greeting, a connection (if necessary), a "pitch" (the purpose for the email), additional details and a closing.

- **Salutation:** A salutation is a greeting used at the beginning of an email. Your salutation should address individual recipients or a group of recipients by name (e.g., "Good morning Nick," "Dear parents" or "Greetings students"). Like your subject line, your salutation should be tailored to the recipients the email is directed at. While more casual greetings like "Hi Nick" or "Hello Amy" are acceptable in most one-on-one email exchanges, a more formal salutation, such as "Greetings" or "Dear" may be more appropriate for groups of recipients or when the tone of the email is more serious in nature.

- **Block Paragraphs:** The body of the email should be written like other forms of public relations writing — in block paragraph form with single spacing between sentences with double spacing between paragraphs.
  - ○ *Connection*: Following your salutation, begin with a one-sentence "connection" that introduces yourself or reminds the recipient how you know him or her. For example, "My name is Leigh Carlson, and I'm the public relations manager for Cupcakes & Candy Boutique in Nashville, Tennessee" or "My name is Leigh Carlson, and we met last year at the PRSA Sunshine District Conference in Tampa, Florida." Note: A "connection" is not always necessary, for example, when emailing someone you regularly communicate with. In these instances, simply omit the connection and continue to your "purpose."
  - ○ *Purpose*: Following your connection (if applicable), state the purpose for your email. Be direct and to-the-point. You should be able to communicate your purpose in one to two sentences: "During the conference, we discussed some potential opportunities for collaboration between your company and Cupcakes & Candy Boutique. I'd like to schedule a meeting for our teams to discuss these exciting opportunities further."
  - ○ *Details*: Once you've stated your purpose, include any additional, relevant details. "Please let us know your availability for an in-person meeting at our Nashville location. We're also happy to come to you if that's more convenient."
  - ○ *Closing*: Similar to the closing of a media pitch, state if — and how — you plan to follow up. A "soft" close leaves any follow up to the recipient. For example, "I look forward to hearing from you. Feel free to call me with any questions." A "hard" close, on the other hand, is more assertive and states how the sender plans to follow up. "I will call you on Monday to follow up with you and make a plan."
    - Your closing should also include your signature sendoff, such as "Best wishes," "Thanks," "Sincerely," "Regards," etc.
- **Email Signature:** Your signature sendoff should be followed by your email signature — the final component of an email message. Email signatures are typically generated by an organization for its employees; however, if you are a student, own your business or are not associated with an organization, you can still create your own professional email signature. For example, for the title line, a student could list "Communication major" and for the organization line, he or she could list their college, university or program. For those who do not have a student email address generated by a college/university or a professional email address generated by a place of work, they can easily create a personal email address through free, Web-based email services like Gmail. Personal email addresses should be simple and professional, such as firstname.lastnight@gmail.com
- Signatures generally follow the structure below, although this structure can be adjusted, and elements can omitted or added depending on organizational style or personal preference.

Name
Title
Department (if applicable)
Name of Organization
Your Phone Number
Your Email Address
Organization's Logo
Organization's Website URL
Organization's Social Media Channels

Note: Students often ask if they can or should include information for their personal social media accounts in their email signatures on or on their online portfolios. While it's customary for an email signature generated by an organization to include the *organization's* social media channels, individuals creating their own signatures for the purposes of sending professional emails probably want to think twice before broadcasting their *own* social media accounts that document their time off the clock, because prospective employers can and will look at them. The exception to this rule is LinkedIn, which is designed for professional networking. Another exception is when social media channels are used as a portfolio of work, for example, a journalist who uses Twitter to share/cover stories or an artist who uses Instagram to showcase his or her work.

❖ PERSPECTIVE FROM THE PROS

By Michael North

When I worked as the director of baseball operations at a community college in Florida, the head coach opened the season with a simple command to the players: "Don't embarrass yourself and don't embarrass the program." This command should guide every email you write.

Write an email today and you probably have your name, email address, cellphone number, fax number, LinkedIn profile, Twitter handle and perhaps an inspirational quote included in your automatic signature. The point is that the recipient of your email knows precisely who you are. Confuse "their" with "there" or "its" with "it's" and the mistake will follow you forever. Even a short reply confirming lunch plans can affect (not effect) your reputation. Don't embarrass yourself.

Your email address is also visible to the recipient. As a student, you probably have a university email address. I am a Miami Hurricane, so my student email address ended with @umiami.edu, meaning every email I wrote reflected back on the University of Miami. When you graduate and get a job, your organization will give you a work email address. Every email you write will reflect back on your employer. Do right by your university, and when the times comes, do right by your employer. Do this by crafting well-written emails that make your organization look good. Don't embarrass the program.

As a professor, I receive hundreds of emails each week from students. One of the main issues I see is confusing text messaging with email communication. Yes, the vast majority of today's emails are written, read and replied to on a cellphone. But that doesn't mean you should use "cuz" or "u" or emojis (I have seen all three). Take the "mail" aspect of email seriously. Hold yourself to the highest standard by proofreading every email you write multiple times.

Lastly, assume that every email you write will become public. Emails are forwarded, copied, or printed all the time. So, use proper grammar, spell every word correctly, adhere to AP style, and edit closely. Do all that and you won't embarrass yourself and you won't embarrass the program.

Format

The formatting used within an email message, including selected fonts, type sizes, colors and signatures, can be determined by organizational style or personal preference. Employees of an organization may be requested to use specific fonts and generated email signatures, among other formatting elements, in order to keep consistency with brand messaging.

Writing for the Web

By Michael North

Search engine optimization appears complex at best, and at worst, scary. While SEO can be a bit technical, remember that public relations is the art and science of reaching a harmony through mutual understanding based upon truth and full information.

As a student learning about public relations, you know that excellent PR begins with research to inform the campaign and ends with tactics that rely just a little on intuition to tailor the persuasive appeal to specific publics. This definition of public relations is useful to keep in mind, because effective SEO also blends the subjectivity of art with the cold analysis of science.

I recently completed a study that examined a year's worth of a large insurance company's search engine advertising campaigns. I specifically analyzed the company's calls-to-action used throughout the year. Calls-to-action that began with "Cover" generated 25 times more clicks than calls-to-action that began with "Insure." The obvious keyword for an insurance company to use would be "Insure" as in: "Insure your boat this summer" or "Insure your property against fire damage." However, "Insure" probably provokes thoughts of expenses and bills. But "Cover" most likely brings about a sense of security or safety. Similarly, "Protect" generated three times more clicks than "Insure." Browsers responded positively to calls-to-action that read: "Protect your loved ones" or "Protect your property this storm season."

Knowing that "Cover" and "Protect" generate more clicks than "Insure" satisfies the science element of the equation. From the art side, looking at "Insure" from a semantic perspective reveals that "Cover" and "Protect" are both near-synonyms. Linguists will tell you that perfect synonyms do not exist because it is inefficient to have multiple words with the exact same meaning in a language. So it is important to find the correct word to resonate positively with browsers. This is where the art aspect plays a role. Some words just produce different reactions such as "Reduce" and "Bundle." Bundling sounds positive, but perhaps it conjures images of adding services that are not needed. "Reduce" – also has a positive connotation – and probably offers a way to reduce costs. It is not surprising, then, that "Reduce" generated four times more clicks than "Bundle." Even though bundling can be an effective sales technique, browsers most likely just wanted to reduce costs in this instance.

This particular insurance company used calls-to-action that began with "Insure" more often than any other even though it generated some of the fewest clicks on average. Far more successful keywords such as "Cover" and "Protect" were not used often enough. This is an example of how effective search engine optimization blends science and art. The numbers indicate HOW specific calls-to-action are performing. But only the art of qualitative research methods such as focus groups and interviews can reveal WHY specific calls-to-action perform better than others. Keep the following in mind when creating content:

Start with internal research: There are generic and specific keywords that relate to every organization. Start by walking around the office asking coworkers for descriptions of the organization and its operations. By doing this, you will hear various words repeated. These are potential keywords. Some of these keywords will be generic meaning that they apply to multiple organizations within the industry, and some keywords will be specific to only your organization. This is the difference between a hamburger and a Whopper Jr. As a content creator for your organization, you'll know most of the generic and specific keywords to use early and often. But conducting a little internal research will reveal additional keywords.

Embrace analytics: Quantitative analysis — otherwise known as math — can be frightening for communication majors. But how else will you know how your keywords are performing? The insurance company used "Insure" more often than any other call-to-action. However, this keyword performed poorly. "Insure" is an obvious keyword to emphasize and should probably be used to cast the occasional wide net, but keywords such as "Cover" and "Protect" performed far better and should have been used more often. Basic analytics will inform your writing and will help you tailor your content to the specific audience you're trying to reach.

Conduct external research: Analytics will not tell you the whole story. Knowing that "Cover" outperforms "Insure" is useful, but you don't know why it's the case. You must conduct external research to fully understand how your keywords resonate with browsers. "Cover" and "Protect" are near-synonyms of "Insure" but all perform differently. Hold a series of focus groups to fully understand the impact that your keywords have on people. Quantitative research tells you the HOW and qualitative research tells you the WHY. Using both triangulates the data thereby revealing the complete picture. Only then will you know the precise keywords to emphasize, the ones to avoid, and why.

In sum, use what you learned about writing mechanics and AP Style when creating content. Always produce perfect content. But in today's internet, you must also carefully word your content so that browsers can find your organization. Think of your homepage as the front door to your organization. But without the URL, browsers will not be able to find the front door. Titling content with "Cover your rental property this winter" or "Reduce your insurance expenses" presents side doors for browsers to enter. Browsers search for their problems and click the best result. Think like a browser and present content that matches how they search.

And don't forget about the research. Start with some internal research to generate a list of keywords. Track how the keywords are performing so you can emphasize the successful keywords and downplay the failures. Seek out browsers to learn why keywords are resonating so you can continue to tweak your content. By researching, creating content that solves problems and using keywords that resonate with browsers, you will drive web traffic to your organization's website — through the side doors that you built, of course.

That's not complex or scary.

Exercise

Exercise 13.1 – Email Message

You are applying for a communications coordinator position at a local nonprofit. Using the email structure reviewed in this chapter and the information below, craft an email to the organization's Human Resources contact that states you are applying for the position.

Next Steps for Veterans is seeking applicants for a communications coordinator position.

Interested candidates should email their resume to Peter Townsend, director of human resources, at peter.townsend@nextsteps4vets.com.

Exercise 13.2 – Search Engine Optimization

Locate Google's "Search Engine Optimization (SEO) Starter Guide" that's available for free online. Read the "Getting Starting" section, focusing specifically on "How do I get my site on Google?"

Next, select an organization that has an existing website. It could be a local nonprofit, a Fortune 500 company or anything in between as long as it has a website you can analyze for the purposes of this exercise.

Imagine that you are the public relations director for this organization and that you've been charged with conducting an SEO audit of the organization's website.

Write a memo to your supervisor with the subject line "SEO audit" that answers these questions:

1.   Is the website showing up on Google?
2.   Does it serve high-quality content to users?
3.   Does local information for the organization show up on Google?
4.   Is the content fast and easy to access on all devices?
5.   Is the website secure?

Use today's date and your instructor's name as the supervisor's name. Print the memo and initial next your name.

References

Newsom, D., & Haynes, J. (2014). *Public Relations Writing: Form & Style* (10th ed.). Boston, MA: Wadsworth.

Smith, R.D. (2017). *Strategic Planning for Public Relations* (5th ed.). New York, NY: Routledge.

Chapter 14

Writing for Social Media

Whitney Lehmann

Purpose

In Chapter 1, we explored the terms *controlled media* and *uncontrolled media*. As a quick refresher, let's examine these definitions, again.

The Public Relations Society of America (PRSA) defines *controlled communication channels* as "Communication channels, media and tools that are under direct control of the sender. Examples include paid advertising, newsletters, brochures, some types of emails, organizational websites and blogs, leaflets, organizational broadcasts and podcasts, intranets, teleconferences and videoconferences, meetings, speeches and position papers" (Glossary of terms, n.d.).

With controlled communication channels, the sender controls the messaging, the tone, the imagery and even the fonts used. For example, think about placing an ad. You pay for the ad space and you control what the ad says, what it looks like, its messaging, its tone, etc.

With *uncontrolled communication channels*, however, this is not the case.

PRSA defines uncontrolled communication channels as "the message-delivery methods that are not under direct control of the company, organization or sender of messages. These channels include newspapers and magazines, radio and television, external websites, externally produced blogs and social media commentary, and externally developed news stories" (Glossary of terms, n.d.).

News releases, media pitches and media advisories are all examples of uncontrolled communication channels. They are public relations tools used to garner media coverage for a client, but the public relations professional has no control over whether this information is used by the media or *how* this information is used by the media.

"Publicity is an uncontrolled method of placing messages because the source does not pay the media for placement and cannot guarantee if or how the material will be used" (Glossary of terms, n.d.).

While *publicity* — information used by news sources because it has news value — is uncontrolled media, social media channels created and maintained by an organization allow it to bypass the media and communicate directly to its various publics with the exact messaging it wants. Whether it be President Donald Trump taking to his Twitter account to address his adversaries; a food manufacturer posting an important update regarding a recall to its Facebook page; a beauty company posting a how-to video to its YouTube channel; or an artist showcasing his or her art on Instagram, these all serve as examples of how an individual or an organization can speak directly to a public or publics with the exact messaging it wants.

While an organization *can* control what and when it posts to its social media accounts, it should be noted that it *cannot* control how publics respond to its social media content or how the organization is talked about on social media, AKA social media commentary. Organizations can, however, be strategic in how they respond to their publics on social media, and public relations professionals are often charged with leading response efforts. Later in this chapter, we'll discuss some tips for engaging in customer service and crisis communications on social media.

Defining Social Media

Before we dive into how to write for social media, let's begin by first defining social media. The term social media is defined differently, depending on whom you ask, as scholars, authors and industry pros and organizations offer a wide variety of definitions, including the below:

- "The term refers to services that allow the sharing of information and content and the formation of communities through online and mobile networks of people" (The Associated Press Stylebook, 2019, p. 365).
- "Social media is the world's largest cocktail party, where people can listen to others talking and join the conversations with other people about any topic of their choice" (Kerpen, 2015, p. 6).
- "Social media does not rely on any particular medium; rather, it is a practice, or set of practices, for using media socially" (Humphreys, 2016, p. 1).
- "A group of Internet-based applications that build on the ideological and technological foundations of web 2.0 and that allow the creation and exchange of User Generated Content" (Kaplan & Haenlein, 2010, p. 61).
- "*Social* is the need that we, as human beings, have to connect with others through companionship via relationships with others in society, either individually or in groups ... The word *media* refers to the channels through which we make connections with others" (Luttrell, 2015, p. 22).

In defining and describing social media, it's also important to note that there are different *types* or categories of social media. While recognized types of social media also differ depending on the source, Hootsuite (2017) groups social media sites into 10 general categories that focus on what people hope to accomplish by using them:

- **Social networks** — Used to connect with people and brands (e.g., Facebook, LinkedIn).
- **Media sharing networks** — Used to share photos, videos, live content and other media (e.g., Instagram, Snapchat, YouTube).
- **Discussion forums** — Used to share news and ideas (e.g., reddit).

- **Bookmarking and content curation networks** — Used to discover, save and share new content (e.g., Pinterest).
- **Consumer review networks** — Used to find and review businesses (e.g., Angie's List, Yelp, TripAdvisor).
- **Blogging and publishing networks** — Used to publish content online (e.g., WordPress, Blogger).
- **Interest-based networks** — Used to share interests and ideas (e.g., Houzz, Goodreads).
- **Social shopping networks** — Used to shop online (e.g., Etsy, Polyvore).
- **Sharing economy networks** — Used to trade goods and services (Airbnb, Uber).
- **Anonymous social networks** — Used to communicate anonymously (Whisper, Ask.fm).

Social Media and Public Relations

Now that we've defined social media and examined different types of social media, where does social media fit into public relations, and, more specifically, into public relations writing?

As public relations professionals, we are tasked with strategically guiding all communications channels for an organization in order to build and maintain mutually beneficial relationships and engage in two-way communication with various publics. In an age of citizen journalism and user generated media, much of these conversations are now taking place publicly through social media.

"For better or worse, a career in PR means handling communications in the public spotlight because of the increasing use of social media. In the wake of democratized content and businesses satisfying the needs of the digitally connected customer, PR had to evolve with a new approach" (Breakenridge, 2012, p 1.).

Breakenridge (2012) identifies eight public relations practices related to social media:

1. Developing social media policies, training and governance.
2. Collaborating with various departments within an organization (PR, Advertising, Marketing, HR, IT, Legal, Sales, etc.) on social media initiatives.
3. Testing the latest technology for greater peer-to-peer communication and remaining up-to-date on social media channels, tools and technology resources.
4. Developing, coordinating and curating content through different social media channels.
5. Building crisis prevention plans to proactively identify negative sentiment and crisis situations on social media channels and respond to them.
6. Observing how audiences connect with their favorite brands and with their peers on social media in order to increase engagement and higher-level interactions.
7. Practicing reputation management by tracking/monitoring social media to respond with immediacy, constant accuracy and transparency.
8. Using measurable objectives and metrics that are tied to higher-level organizational goals.

What these practices — and others — tell us, as communications professionals, is that simply having a presence on social media is not enough. In order for an organization to truly be successful in its social media efforts, it must also be strategic.

"In the world of public relations, marketing, and communication, it is more important than ever that professionals have a strategic understanding of how to utilize social media effectively" (Kim, 2016, p. 1).

As new media continue to evolve and transform the field of public relations, public relations professionals must evolve along with them.

"Whether it's young professionals entering the workforce or seasoned practitioners, the competent use of information technologies is a necessary skill, which has become a part of the PR professional's daily practice" (Breakenridge, 2012, p. 2).

Communicating Across Social Media Channels

Public relations practitioners are tasked with writing for all types of social media operated by an organization. A typical day on the job might involve posting an important news update to the company's Facebook page, answering consumers' questions on Twitter, live streaming an event on Instagram live, crafting a Q&A with an exec for a blog post, creating a how-to video for the company's YouTube channel, responding to a customer complaint on Yelp, or promoting a job opportunity on LinkedIn.

While writing for each specific category of social media is beyond the scope of this book, it is important to establish that public relations professionals need to be strategic in writing not just for different types of social media but for all social media sites in general.

As a public relations pro, it's your job to know the inherent purpose of any social sites your organization has a presence on in order to use them strategically with content. Whereas Facebook posts are typically informational in nature, tweets tend to be used for updates or breaking news. Instagram, Snapchat and YouTube tell stories through photos and videos while blog posts explore a topic in great detail through the written word. Yelp, Angie's List and TripAdvisor are for creating and sharing reviews, and Pinterest allows users to curate content around specific topics. And so on.

Social media managers also need to be privy to the "rules of the road" for social media sites, including any limitations, so that they can adjust their writing accordingly. For example, while Facebook's character limit for posts is in the tens of thousands, Tweets are limited to 280 characters. Instagram does not hyperlink URLs in captions or comments, but it does allow users to include a clickable link in user bios (e.g., "Click link in bio to learn more"). On Snapchat, we instead attach links to snaps and direct friends to "swipe up."

It's also important to know the lingo associated with different social sites. Facebook, Instagram and LinkedIn have "posts," Twitter has "tweets," Snapchat has "snaps" and Pinterest has "pins." Facebook and LinkedIn have "pages" to differentiate from personal profiles, YouTube has "channels" that categorize content by "playlists," Pinterest has "boards" and Snapchat has "stories." Facebook and

Instagram now have "stories," too. Facebook pages have "followers," but Facebook profiles have "friends." LinkedIn profiles have "connections," LinkedIn pages have "followers" and YouTube channels have "subscribers."

For a full breakdown of the most widely used social media sites, check out Dave Kerpen's book *Likeable Social Media, Third Edition: How to Delight Your Customers, Create an Irresistible Brand, & Be Generally Amazing on All Social Networks that Matter* (2019).

❖ PERSPECTIVE FROM THE PROS

By Michael North

Legend has it Ernest Hemingway once won a bet by crafting a six-word story that went: "For Sale: Baby Shoes, Never Worn." Whether Hemingway actually wrote that story is beside the point. The power of this six-word story stems from its brevity, unusualness and the unknown. High-quality social media writing incorporates these three components.

Social media writing needs to be brief. In a time when a five-minute YouTube video is bordering on long, social media users like GIFs, two-line memes and Snapchat videos measured in seconds. Perhaps nothing epitomizes this more than Twitter's original 140-character limit, now expanded to 280 characters. Twitter's hook is its character limit, which forces users to get to the point by trimming the excess. Even Facebook posts generate more engagement when the text clocks in at about 100 characters.

Social media writing needs to be interesting. Unusualness, or bizarreness to some, is an accepted news value. In other words, a story about a dog biting a man will be ignored, but a story about a man going around biting dogs could go viral. With so much content produced every day, your writing must grab attention. Not everything is worth posting, but when something unusual does happen, promote it on social media.

Social media writing needs to convey a sense of the unknown. Digital content exists to generate engagement in the form of likes, shares, retweets and clicks. If the digital content presents all the information, the user will continue to scroll and they won't give you that engagement. But if the digital content teases valuable information found only by clicking the link, your content will generate engagement. Don't give all the information, but tease that valuable information awaits behind the link found within the social media post.

"For Sale: Baby Shoes, Never Worn" dates back to the time of classified ads in the newspaper, but it also could be the perfect tweet. Hemingway did not ramble on with a story about how the cobbler selected the perfect strips of leather and then crafted the baby shoes with love. He did not bore with an ordinary tale about hand-me-down baby shoes passed on to a newborn sibling. And Hemingway did not tell why the baby shoes went unused thereby allowing the reader a chance to use their imagination.

Distill your point down to its essence when creating social media content. Post something interesting to rise above the digital fray. Present the promise of something valuable to come.

Be brief. Be unusual. Tease the unknown.

Writing for Social Media

While each social media site comes with its own "rules" for writing, there are also some general rules that can and should be applied when writing for social media:

- **Be conversational.** Social media is about being social. Write in first/second person ("we" and "you"). Ask questions to generate conversation and reply to followers' questions/comments within 24 hours.
- **Know thy voice.** Your tone — be it formal, playful, serious, witty, whimsical or anything in between — should be consistent across all your social channels in order to maintain brand identity. Your "voice" should also be appropriate for the industry your organization belongs to (e.g., academia versus a liquor company).
- **Stick to Associated Press (AP) Style.** Use AP Style as your guide when crafting captions and posts but make exceptions when necessary (e.g., using accepted abbreviations with Twitter due to character limits).
- **Use proper punctuation and grammar.** While conversational, social media writing should still adhere to proper punctuation and grammar (refer to AP Style's "Punctuation & Grammar" section). That said, allow exceptions when the content calls for it (e.g., "How 'bout them Canes?").
- **Incorporate handles/hashtags into captions.** Use handles to engage with other users and hashtags to join conversations (e.g., "Looking for a fun and productive way to spend your summer? Apply to our #nsuicecream program that's taking place on @nsuflorida campus July 16–20.").
- **Follow accepted channel practices for hyperlinks:**
  - Snapchat: "Swipe up" for hyperlinks
  - Instagram: "Click the link in our bio"
  - Twitter: use Bitly to shorten links when needed
- **Include a Call to Action (CTA):** Include a call to action ("Swipe Up," "Learn more," "Apply today!" "Donate now," etc.) tied to organizational goals. CTAs can also be used to keep the conversation going (e.g., "Let us know what you think") or to garner User Generated Content that your organization can feature on its accounts (with permission). For instance, "Share your best summer pics with #socialsummer for a chance to see them featured on our accounts."

❖ PERSPECTIVE FROM THE PROS

By Kim Cohane

Before posting a great image or video on social media, you will want to craft an eye-catching caption. A well-crafted caption and visual can stop a viewer from scrolling past your content and get your audience to engage with your brand. Companies and organizations sometimes forget social media creates an opportunity for two-way conversations, not just a one-directional blast of their latest news or product update.

You can increase engagement with a caption simply by asking them to join the conversation! A few ways you can get the conversation going include:

- Ask the audience to chime in. "What do you think about _____?"
- Ask them to check-in from their location. This works well if your audience is spread out geographically, your audience is traveling (e.g., spring break) and during seasonal events when audiences can share how hot or cold it is at their location.
- Share their reaction or respond to your post in a GIF or emoji. Audiences love to have fun on social media and this is a quick way to build a fun conversation around your brand's content.
- Create polls to get valuable audience feedback on just about anything.
- Ask simple Yes/No questions to let them vote on a topic, product, or feature your organization offers or will consider offering in the future.

Remember to document and measure your engagement metrics! Test some of these social media conversational starters by adding them to your content calendar and adjust them based on audience feedback.

Customer Service and Crisis Communications

Social media's two-way interactive nature and ability to communicate instantaneously makes it the ultimate tool for customer service and crisis communications.

Customer Service

When it comes to customer service, one thing is certain — customers want to know that they've been heard.

"No human being is perfect, and therefore no organization is either. Your company will surely make errors, and now, thanks to social networks, the whole world can easily find out about those mistakes. But you also have the ability to show the world how responsive a company you are" (Kerpen, 2015, p. 89).

Whether you're answering product questions or responding to a complaint or compliment, follow these tips for successful interactions:

- **Address the person by name.** Interactions should be personal, and therefore, address the person by name (e.g., "Hi Robert" or "Thanks for reaching out, Robert!").
- **Respond to questions ASAP**. Although the standard for responding to social media inquiries is 24 hours, reply sooner when possible.
- **Adhere to the Do-Not-Delete Rule.** "Unless a comment is obscene, profane, or bigoted, or contains someone's personal and private information, it should never be deleted from a social network site" (Kerpen, 2015, p. 81). Deleting a follower's negative comment sends the message that your organization doesn't care. Remember, customers want to know that they've been heard. While deleting a nasty comment may seem a quick fix, it could actually incite the person even more.
- **Go straight to the source.** When a question or complaint relates to a specific department (e.g., Food & Beverage, Legal, Finance, Security, Manufacturing, etc.), go straight to the source. Communicate the question or concern with the department head to get any needed clarification or detail before responding.
- **Acknowledge complaints when warranted.** While not all complaints or negative comments warrant a response (e.g., those that are unfounded, obscene, profane, hostile, etc.), respond to those that do. Be sympathetic, be apologetic, and when possible, offer a solution to fix the problem or a way to make it up to them: "We're sorry to hear you had a bad experience. We hope you'll consider dining with us again soon and enjoy a dessert on us!"
- **Always acknowledge compliments.** If followers take the time to comment something positive about your brand, take the time to reply and show your appreciation. A simple "Thanks, Paige!" or "We're so happy to hear you're enjoying our product" goes a long way and helps to build brand loyalty. You can, of course, "like" a comment, too.
- **Take the conversation offline when necessary.** Take heated conversations offline and out of the public arena by asking the person to direct message you.

Crisis Communications

Public relations professionals can also use social media to communicate with an organization's publics during a time of crisis. In the event of a crisis or emergency situation, organizations need to communicate updates quickly and directly with its publics, and today many are turning to Twitter to get their news out. "For organizations and emergency response agencies, it's the fastest way to disseminate the most critical information to the largest amount of people in the shortest amount of time" (Crisis Response Toolkit, n.d., para. 1).

While public relations professionals charged with leading an organization's crisis response on Twitter and other social media channels should have a comprehensive crisis management plan in place, the tips below can help guide a response on social media (Crisis Response, n.d.):

- **Designate a crisis response team/person.** Communications teams should designate a specific person (and a back-up person) to lead the crisis response on social media channels.
- **During a crisis situation, post only critical information.** Suspend all regularly programmed content and post only critical information. #Mondaymotivation is not only inappropriate during a crisis/emergency situation, but it will also dilute your messaging and make you look insensitive to your followers.
- **Consult the proper authorities for determining what information to share.** Before tweeting, double check with the appropriate person to ensure the information can be made public.
- **Establish a hashtag for the incident.** Create an appropriate hashtag for the crisis and ensure that all employees, members of the media and concerned parties are aware of it.
- **Direct followers to where they can get more information.** Direct followers to additional sources of information once available. "For more information about the recall, view the press release posted to our website here: www.organization.com/recall."
- **After the state of emergency has passed, continue to share updates as needed.** Help your followers get organized and recover by continuing to share important updates related to the crisis.

Exercises
Exercise 14.1 – Social Media Captions

You are the public relations director for Farmhouse Foods. Use the information below to craft a tweet announcing the brand's new line of flavored milks on the Farmhouse Foods official Twitter account. Remember, tweets are 280 characters or less.

- The Holy Cow! flavored-milk line will be available in select grocery stores and organic markets beginning April 1, 2020.
- The line is USDA certified organic and features low-fat milk in three flavors: chocolate, strawberry and vanilla.
- Holy Cow! milks will be available by the half gallon and as 8-ounce single servings that come in a case of eight.
- All Holy Cow! milks are free of artificial flavors and colors and contain DHA Omega-3 to support brain and eye health.
- More information about the Holy Cow! flavored-milk line is available at www.farmhousefoods.com/holycow
- Follow Holy Cow! on Facebook, Twitter and Instagram @holycowmilks
- Join the Holy Cow! conversation using the hashtag #holycow

Exercise 14.2 – Customer Service

A Farmhouse Foods Twitter follower, @JennaParker, replies to your tweet and wants to know where she can find a store near her that will carry the Holy Cow! flavored-milk line. Using the customer service tips provided in this chapter, craft a reply that directs the follower to a full list of participating stores at www.farmhousefoods.com/holycow/ storelocator

References

Crisis Response (n.d.). Retrieved from https://about.twitter.com/content/dam/about-twitter/values/twitter-for-good/Twitter-Crisis-Response-One-Pager.pdf

Facebook newsroom. (n.d.). Retrieved from https://newsroom.fb.com/company-info/

Foreman, C. (2017, June 20). 10 types of social media and how each can benefit your business. https://blog.hootsuite.com/types-of-social-media/

Glossary of terms. (n.d.). Retrieved from www.prsa.org/glossary-of-terms/

Humphreys, A. (2006). *Social Media: Enduring Principles.* New York: Oxford University Press.

Kaplan, A.M., & Haenlein, M. (2010). Users of the world, unite! The challenges and opportunities of social media. *Business Horizons, 53*(1), 59–68.

Kerpen, D. (2015). *Likeable Social Media: How to Delight Your Customers, Create an Irresistible Brand, and Be Amazing on Facebook, Twitter, LinkedIn, Instagram, Pinterest and More* (2nd ed.). United States: McGraw-Hill Education.

Kerpen, D. (2019). *Likeable Social Media, Third Edition: How to Delight Your Customers, Create an Irresistible Brand, & Be Generally Amazing on All Social Networks that Matter* (3rd ed.). United States: McGraw-Hill Education.

Kim, C.M. (2016). *Social Media Campaigns: Strategies for Public Relations and Marketing.* New York: Routledge.

Luttrell, R. (2005). *Social Media: How to Engage, Share, and Connect.* Lanham, MD: Rowman & Littlefield.

The Associated Press (2019). *The Associated Press Stylebook 2019 and Briefing on Media Law.* New York: The Associated Press.

Business and Executive Communications

Chapter 15

Letters and Memos

Whitney Lehmann

Chapter 15 kicks off the section of this text that explores various forms of business and executive communications that public relations professionals regularly engage with when communicating with internal and external publics on behalf of an organization.

Letters

Purpose

Business letters are documents used to communicate a variety of types of messages to a specific individual on behalf of an organization, including (Carden & Zappala, 2010; Marsh, Guth, & Poovey Short, 2012; Newsom & Haynes, 2014):

- General information, such as announcements and updates (e.g., upcoming event or decision made).
- Good news or information that will please the recipient (e.g., scholarship award letter or promotion letter).
- Bad news or information the recipient doesn't want to hear (e.g., credit card denial).
- Thank you (e.g., thanking someone for a donation).
- Apology (e.g., responding to a dissatisfied customer).
- Acceptance or resignation (e.g., accepting a job offer or resigning from a position).
- Sales information about goods and services (e.g., insurance policy solicitation).
- Request for information (e.g., request for documents or public records).
- Request for consideration (e.g., cover letter applying for a job).
- Request for immediate action (e.g., request to update contact information).

While letters are primarily directed at individuals outside of an organization, letters can also be used to communicate with individuals within an organization, for example, a resignation letter addressed to a supervisor or a scholarship letter addressed to a student enrolled at a university.

Format

Letters are typically printed on an organization's stationery, including its letterhead and envelopes, and mailed to an individual. The standard letter size in the United States is 8.5 x 11 inches. Organizational stationery is often designed in house by a publications team, with letterhead produced in print and digital formats.

Although letters can be emailed, formal business letters that are printed on an organization's letterhead, placed in an envelope and mailed are generally more appropriate when communicating information to individuals outside of an organization. The type of information being communicated should also help to determine whether a letter should be printed and mailed or sent via email. While information casual in nature, such as a Homeowners Association announcing its annual meeting, can be communicated via email, more serious information, such as an insurance provider denying a policy holder's claim, should be reserved for print letters.

Letters are usually one page in length but can be longer when necessary. Sales letters that explain a product or service in great detail, for example, are often more than one page.

The typeface/font used on a letter should be easy to read. Times New Roman is a popular serif typeface and Calibri is a popular sans serif option. Script typefaces should be avoided, as they are not suitable for large amounts of body text.

The type size should also be readable. Standard type size is 11 or 12 point, although this ultimately depends on the specific typeface being used.

Structure

A business letter contains the following elements in this order:

Header

The letterhead for an organization has a header and/or footer area that contains the organization's official logo, address and telephone number. The telephone number can be followed by an email address or website, although this information is optional.

The logo and accompanying elements of the letterhead may be centered aligned, left aligned or right aligned, depending on the organization's style preference.

When writing letters not on organizational stationery, such as a cover letter for a job application, replace the organizational header with your own name, address, phone number and email address.

Date

A date should follow the letterhead that indicates today's date (the date the letter was written). Dates should be fully written out and include the month, day and year. For example, July 19, 2019.

Recipient Information

The next block of information should contain the recipient's information, including his or her name, title, organization, the organization's street address and the organization's city, state and zip code. The individual's home address may also be used in place of an organizational address.

Salutation

The next three blocks of information — the salutation, the body and the closing — follow the same structure as media pitches (Chapter 3) and email (Chapter 13) but with some modifications.

The salutation — the greeting — used with a business letter is generally more formal than the salutation used with a media pitch or email (e.g., "Hi Susan"). Letters typically use the salutation "Dear" and address the person by full name, including any prefixes to indicate title, such as "Dr." or suffixes, such as "Jr." Another difference is that the salutations for letters use courtesy titles, such as Mr. and Mrs., unlike pitches and email, which avoid them.

Body

The body of the letter should be written with block paragraphs and contain the following components:

- *Purpose*: The first sentence/paragraph should communicate the purpose of the email. Be direct and to-the-point. "This letter is to inform you of a product recall for inclined infant sleepers produced by Lullaby Baby Inc. The products being recalled include the Rocking Cradle Sleeper (model number LBI2004) and Slumber Sounds Rocker (model number LBI2009)."
- *Details*: Once you've stated your purpose, include any additional, relevant details. "This recall has been initiated due to concerns that infants sleeping in them could roll over and suffocate. No injuries have been reported, so this recall is precautionary. Parents and caretakers are urged to discontinue use of the infant sleepers immediately and contact Lullaby Baby Inc. for a $100 refund voucher."
- *Next Steps/More Information*: Similar to a media pitch, state if — and how — you plan to follow up or if you request any action on behalf of the recipient. The closing can also direct recipients to sources of additional information. "Customers can request their refund vouchers by calling the Lullaby Baby Inc. recall hotline at 555-555-5555 or emailing @inclinesleeperrecall@lullaby.com."

Closing

Your closing should include a professional sendoff, such as "Sincerely," "Best Regards," "Thank You," "Best Wishes," etc.

Signature

The closing is followed by the sender's signature. While a penned signature is preferred, organizations can also utilize stamps and digital signatures for mass mailings.

Sender Name/Title

Include the sender's name and title below his or her signature. Including a typed name and title avoids any confusion caused by an illegible signature.

Business Letter Template

Organization's Logo
Organization's Street Address
City, State ZIP CODE
555-555-5555

Date
Recipient's Name
Recipient's Title
Name of Organization
Street Address for Recipient's Organization (or home address)
City, State ZIP CODE
Salutation,

Business letters should be written in block paragraph form with single spacing between sentences and double spacing between paragraphs. The first paragraph should state the purpose of the letter.

Once the purpose is stated, subsequent paragraphs should communicate any relevant details. Letters are usually one page in length but can be longer when necessary. Sales letters that explain a product or service in great detail, for example, are often more than one page.

A final paragraph should state any next steps, including if you plan to follow up or if you request any action on behalf of the recipient. This final paragraph can also direct the recipient to sources of additional information, such as a website, phone number, email address or social media accounts.

Closing,
Sender's Signature

Sender's Name
Sender's Title

❖ PERSPECTIVE FROM THE PROS

By Megan Fitzgerald

People underestimate the power of a cover letter. While you may spend time and money putting together the perfect interview outfit, your cover letter breezes through the company's door long before you do.

The cover letter truly makes the first impression. And, like any first impression, it can be lasting. A strong cover letter should be carefully tailored and properly put together. It should take your resume and bring it to life by telling a story — one that demonstrates why you are the best fit for that specific position. Avoid taking the one-size-fits-all approach with cover letters. Each position you apply for should have a letter written specifically with that position in mind. Your letter should show that you have researched the company and highlight why you are, in fact, the best candidate for that position.

Your cover letter should also put your best foot forward and sending a letter that is rushed has mistakes or typos is a serious misstep. I still remember the sinking feeling I got when, right after graduating college, I realized that I had sent a cover letter with a typo to a magazine for an assistant editor position. It was a small mistake. One little misspelled word typed too quickly and not caught by spell check. But, cover letters say much about you. And, mine told the story of someone seeking an editing position who did not proofread well. I did not receive an interview and, while I can't be certain it was due to my error, I am certain that I did not make an ideal first impression, and my perfect interview outfit hung in my closet longer than I would have liked.

Memorandum

Purpose

While business letters are used primarily to communicate with external publics, memoranda, also known as memos, are used to communicate with internal publics. Think of memos as internal business letters.

Another difference between letters and memos is that memos are often directed at a group of people — such as employees, staff, board members, etc. — unlike letters, which are directed at individuals.

"Memos are intended to increase communication within an organization. They are usually meant to inform readers of a particular issue. They can help to open up the lines of communication, allowing a number of people to be aware of several issues" (Diggs-Brown, 2013, p. 208).

Like letters, memos are used to communicate different types of information, including (Diggs-Brown, 2013; Zappala & Carden, 2010):

- new developments
- upcoming events
- confirmation of decisions and agreements
- program/event updates and itineraries
- short reports
- brief proposals
- meeting outlines

- notes
- reminders
- and more

Format

Like letters, memos are also composed on an organization's letterhead. Memos are brief, typically a few paragraphs but no longer than a page. Although memos were originally printed on paper and distributed through office mail, today they are sent mostly through email.

Structure

Memos have a distinct structure that features the following elements:

Header

The header of a memo contains the organization's official logo or seal, address and telephone number. The telephone number can be followed by additional information, such as a fax number, an email address or website. As mentioned previously with letters, these elements may appear in a header, footer or both. For example, the organization's logo or seal may appear in the header area while the full address, phone number, fax number and/or website may appear in the footer area.

Following the letterhead is the word "Memorandum" or "Memo," often written in all capital letters in a larger type size.

In addition to the letterhead and the title, the header area of a standard memo contains these four items: To, From, Date and Subject. Let's examine each below:

- To: The name and title of the individual (e.g., John Smith, vice president of finance) or the name of a group of individuals (e.g., Sunshine State University Employees) the memo is written to.
- From: The sender's name and title (e.g., Barbara Davis, President and CEO).
- Date: The date the memo is distributed, including the day of the week, the month, the day and year (e.g., Friday, May 17, 2019).
- Subject: A brief description of the memo's subject/contents in as few words as possible (e.g., Bonus Awards).

While the order of the four items presented above is standard for most memos, it could also be altered for organizational style or preference. Line spacing between the four items should be at least 1.5 to make the categories readable.

It should also be noted that the "Subject" category can also be replaced with "Re:" — meaning "Regarding" — and that printed memos typically include handwritten initials from the sender next to his or her name.

Body

The body of a memo should follow block paragraph form with single spacing between paragraphs and double spacing between paragraphs. The information should be communicated concisely in as few paragraphs as possible using inverted pyramid with content organized from the most important details to the least important details.

Unlike letters, emails and media pitches, memos do not conclude with a closing such as "Sincerely" or "Best Regards." They simply end after the final paragraph.

Memo Template

Organization's Logo or Seal

MEMO

To: Recipient's name, title

From: Sender's name, title <include hand-written initials on printed memos>

Date: Day of the week, full date (e.g., Saturday, Aug. 3, 2019)

Subject: Describe the subject matter in as few words as possible

The body of a memo should follow block paragraph form with single spacing between paragraphs and double spacing between paragraphs. The information should be communicated concisely in as few paragraphs as possible using inverted pyramid with content organized from the most important details to the least important details.

Unlike letters, emails and media pitches, memos do not use a closing such as "Sincerely" or "Best." They simply conclude with the final paragraph.

Organization's Street Address
City, State ZIP CODE
Telephone: 555-555-5555 | Fax: 555-555-5555
www.website.com

Exercises

Exercise 15.1 – Cover Letter

Locate a job listing for a position you aspire to have in the field of communications. Using the letter template from this chapter, craft a cover letter tailored to the position that outlines your experience and why you are a strong candidate for the job.

Exercise 15.2 – Memorandum

Locate an example of a memo online. Compare and contrast it with the memo structure and template presented in this chapter. Next, write a memo to your instructor with today's date detailing your findings in 500 words or less. Print your memo and initial it. Print and attach the memo example to the back.

Chapter 16

Speech Writing

Michael Laderman

A natural progression for a communications leader and executive is being asked to represent the CEO of a company, organization or institution. And in doing so, it is being asked to essentially be not the name and not the face, per se, but rather the *words* and the *actions* behind the name and behind the face of those who are those respective leaders.

For example, have you ever bothered to think that many of the greatest speeches that have ever been written and given were not necessarily written by those who spoke them? Rather, there is a very good chance — more likely than not — that those respective speeches were actually written and penned by somebody just like you and me.

Somebody in a communications role, charged with writing the thoughts of not only the leader, but understanding the thoughts of what the audience needs and wants to hear.

Organizations throughout the globe have people hired specifically for these roles.

Even organizations that you would never think would need to have a publicist handling their messaging … they do.

When things go wrong at a lawyer's office, many a time, a PR company steps in. [Lawyers will typically understand that they win the battles within the court of law; but PR professionals win the battles within the court of public opinion.] It was a crisis communications team that stepped in when the Exxon Valdez oil spill occurred. When the Space Shuttle Columbia disintegrated upon entry, it was NASA's communications team that handled its messaging.

And when a president of a corporation or politician of most any type looks to speak to a gathering, it is, most likely, a publicist who writes their words.

Now, this is not to insinuate that the leader will never get their hands dirty with this. This is not to say that the leader will not also write words.

Some will be more involved than others.

I have had the pleasure, honor and distinction of being the words, and in a sense, the voice of five leaders at major universities, each one of them accepting my words as theirs, with each one of them being as different as the other. Each one of them, though, holding amazing positions of power in various levels in various cities.

The most prestigious, nationally and internationally that I represented was Clemson University's president, James P. Clements. He was a joy to work for, and to work with, because he was willing to have the conversation of what he wanted to say. Prior to events that he was speaking at, I would sit with him and go over the main points that he was looking to make. I would be prepared to suggest my own talking points, per my research and thoughts of what key points were needed to be made. Based on that initial discussion, we would end up with a speech that would be sent to President Clements for his review.

And more often than not, right away, he would send me corrections as to what changes he had to make. There were times with President Clements that nothing at all was changed. And other times, it was a consistent back and forth.

The key on that is putting yourself, as the writer, in the position of the speaker — in this case, President Clements — literally being him in *his* voice, trying to speak as best as possible as *he* speaks with the kind of verbiage that *he* specifically uses.

My very first project for president Clements was distributed on his second day on the job as president of Clemson University — January 1, 2014. Clemson University's football team was in Miami for the Orange Bowl game against The Ohio State University. As then-Clemson's director of academic communications, I was tasked with being the president's right hand PR-wise for that trip. Every event he was at, I was at, helping to give guidance with what he should say at each event, what pictures he should take, and who he should take them with.

The first main project on his behalf, though, leading up to his first days at president, was writing an op-ed for *The Miami Herald* — on his behalf — about how Clemson University encourages collaboration between universities.

I spent hours and days researching speeches that President Clements had given before, to get the gist of not only the words he uses, but the tone in which he speaks them. I reached out to his then-former PR office at West Virginia University for any additional background information I could gather.

And then I did not sit down in front of my computer, but rather, stood in front of a mirror, hit record on my phone's voice recorder app, and proceeded to speak the words that I not only felt President Clements would say, but those that I thought he should say within the space of the op-ed.

When the first draft was complete, I sent it to him via email, as he had not yet begun to work on campus the week prior to traveling to Miami. And he responded quickly via email as to whatever changes he had.

For our first go-around, there were not many. A paragraph here, a paragraph there. But for the most part, the article stayed as is and as was.

So I went to my first meeting with President Clements, not in-person, but rather via email discussing an op-ed, of which, I'm sure from his perspective, a stranger put words in his mouth.

We met formally, face-to-face, for the first time in Miami at his very first Orange Bowl event on December 31, 2013. And from there, it was one of the best working relationships — if not *the* best working relationship — with a leader I ever had.

Now, by the time President Clements and I first met, I already had 15-plus years of experience directly representing campus and organizational leaders. Thus, I already knew the nuances of what it took to be the voice of a leader.

What truly prepared me to do that so well with President Clements was my role 14 years earlier.

As a then-young 31-year-old, being named Nova Southeastern University's associate director of public affairs, marketing and advertising, I was charged with being the university's leader of overall media relations. I was quickly given the additional task of being the voice behind President Ray Ferrero Jr.

President Ferrero was an intimidating individual to virtually all on campus who did not know him. And then, even when you got to know him, his persona of being matter of fact, and extremely professional to the T, kept the intimidation factor going. Whether he wanted that perception or not was always unclear. But as I quickly learned from him, as a leader of somebody in charge of 10,000 employees, and 30,000 students, it's not a bad thing to have.

From a communications perspective, you learn to adapt to it. And you learn to embrace it. You never complain about it. You never complain about leadership styles, because every leader you are with will have a different style.

President Ferrero's style was that of straight and to-the-point.

And so, as that young 31-year-old who, from spending the previous four years as assistant athletic director in charge of sports information and event management, was given the promotion to oversee media relations university-wide, it was, indeed, intimidating to suddenly be not only in the same room as President Ferrero, but at the table right next to him, giving him direction on what to say, when to say it, and how to say it.

I was the voice and words of every single major speech and presentation he were to give between December 1999 and November 2003.

Here is what made President Ferrero so special and so memorable.

He not only welcomed me in his way, but he encouraged me in his way. He accepted me, not once looking down at me as a young, inexperienced communicator but, rather, someone who knew what he was doing [no matter the age], which made my job easier.

Still, becoming President Ferrero was, many a time, nerve-wracking. Because President Ferrero, with his straight-and-narrow/to-the-point style, was very picky and choosy with his words. Thus, his speeches had to reflect that style and tone.

His way of giving speeches paved the way though for how I would work with all other leaders with their respective forms of communication.

Every speech, 24-point font size. All capital letters. Hyphens and colons to indicate pauses. Never end a page in mid-sentence, no matter how blank the bottom of the page would look. Number each page. Print single-sided pages. Place each page in a glossy page protector. Four binders prepared for each speech. Two binders to him, one to his administrative assistant and one for me.

Fast forward to my role as assistant vice president for communications and marketing and university relations with Barry University.

There, I worked alongside two university presidents — each one more different than the other.

Sister Jeanne O'Laughlin, OP Ph.D., was one who did everything off the cuff. In my one year of working alongside her, there was not one event in which she asked for me to help writing her speech.

I remember the very first time there was such an opportunity to do so. I approached Sister Jeanne and asked her if she would like me to write the first draft of her remarks for an event that she was going to represent Barry University at. She looked at me, smiled, and said, "Michael, I've been doing this for 20 years. I don't need remarks."

Her successor, sister Linda Bevilacqua, OP Ph.D., was different in her own way.

Sister Linda was the president who would ask for her remarks to be completely written out. But she would more so ask them to be written out not because she wanted to use them, but rather she would use them as a base for what she, then, would want to write about.

So speeches would be sent to her, and she would do a complete rewrite of my remarks.

She would then send her version of the speech back to me for review, and any changes that I might want to make.

It was a unique system, but one that worked for the president.

And that is what you must always remember. It is not about you, or your feelings, when writing remarks for a leader of an organization or an institution. It is about them, and what they are comfortable with. I never took any offense from sister Linda not wanting to use my remarks. Because she trusted me enough to review her remarks that were based on my initial remarks, and then would have me come down to her office once those remarks were finalized in order to help prep her for how the remarks would sound when she spoke the words in front of an audience.

That is above all what you need to remember when being asked to do this part of your communications role. Remember and understand that it is not about you. Everything to do with this responsibility has to do with what the person you are representing needs from you, whether it is words, or helping them with their actions to deliver their words.

For 20 plus years, I would consistently tell my teams that, in their communication roles, they have a bull's eye on them. It's on their chest, their back, their arms, their forehead — that every part of their body has a bull's eye on it. This is because, as a communications expert, you are in the forefront of the words and actions that the organization you represent says and delivers, especially when you represent the chief executive officer.

In this role, you will be asked to write speeches and every other form of communication that represents your organization and its leadership. You will be tasked with writing letters, memos and social media posts. You will be asked to write the scripts for the university president, or museum director, or chair of the board of trustees, for whatever it is they do, wherever it is they go. You will be the words of those leaders in the times of crisis and when things are going smoothly. You will be asked to help write annual reports, letters to the editor, newspaper op-eds and responses to articles that are either good and/or bad.

And through it all, every single step of the way, you need to put yourself in their respective shoes. And I assure you of this: There is not one size shoe that all leaders wear.

Every single leader is different with what their needs and requests are. It is your job and your responsibility to adhere and adjust and adapt quickly to what your respective leader and boss and director needs from you.

As a communicator, you will be there to directly assist them with their words and their actions and their delivery. It is, and can be, the most intense position in an organization. But know that when you reach that point — where you are the one who is asked to write the words and thoughts and feelings and delivery of a respective leader — that you have made it to a point that many others wish that they had achieved.

Use your experience, use what is in your heart, and use what you know to be right, when penning, writing and imagining the words that your leader is asking you to come up with. Just remember – they are not your words. They are theirs. But do your best impression of them to assist them, and your words will be the ones to help motivate, comfort, encourage and rally audiences throughout.

Speech Writing Template

Every speech should be written and formatted the way the speaker is comfortable with. Personalize the speech. Make it tell a story. Make it flow as though the person talking is having a conversation, not just reading bullet points.

Speeches should be structured with a strong introduction, middle and closing.

Formatting Tips:

- *Use an easy-to-read typeface and a large type size, such as 24 (depending on the typeface).*
- *Use a minimum spacing of 1.5.*
- *Use headers in various areas, so the speaker knows what topic they are moving into.*
- *Use bullet points for speech copy.*
- *Use page numbers on all pages.*

Notes:

- *Speeches are not necessarily written in AP Style. Numbers lower than 10 are not spelled out; they are written numerically, as they are easier for the speaker to see when reading.*
- *Some speakers may prefer that speeches be written in all capital letters. Adhere to the speaker's preference.*
- *Template prompts in italics are for instructional purposes and should be deleted.*

Title of Speech or Name of Event
Date
Include the day of the week and the full date (e.g., Monday, Aug. 5, 2019)
Insert your own headers.

Introduction and acknowledgments

- Thank you – Mr. Chairman – for that very kind introduction.
- And – thank you all – for being here this afternoon!

Use hyphens in the middle of sentences, instead of commas; it's easier for the speaker to see when reading fast.

A little bit about [speaker]

- Since this may be the 1st time I've met many of you – let me tell you a little bit about myself – and why I am so excited to be here.
- <Insert more background information here>

Highlights

- We have a lot to be thankful for – and – a lot of successes to highlight. ☺

Emoticons are good; they will help tell the speaker know how they should react.

- <Insert highlights here>

Closing Remarks

- Thank you, again, for your continued support. And – thank you for inviting me – to be with you today.
- Goodnight and God bless.

Notes:

Will be introduced by Sen. John Smith.

About 100 people expected.

Will be a podium and microphone.

Notes at the end of the speech are placed here purposefully, so that the speaker sees quick and general information of what to expect.

Exercise

Exercise 16.1 – Speech Writing

Write a three- to four-minute speech for someone you know.

Make up an event for a friend or colleague of yours — or choose an event that they are already going to. Now, imagine that they, themselves, are the featured presenter, giving the main "remarks" of the event's presentation.

They have been told that the speech must fit in the three- to four-minute range. It cannot be less; it cannot be more.

Your job is to put yourself in the presenter's place and pen their words for them.

But the job doesn't end there. You must also format it appropriately with:

- *appropriate readable font size*
- *line spacing*
- *page numbers*

Tips:

- *Ensure that your speech has a strong introduction, middle and closing.*
- *Find an actual event, so you can appropriately put facts, figures and general information into your speech.*

Writing for Events

Chapter 17

Talking Points and Run of Show

Whitney Lehmann

Chapters 15 and 16 examined how public relations professionals are often tasked with crafting speeches, letters, memos and other forms of business communications for executives and other key people within an organization.

The next section of this text examines public relations writing within an event context. Let's begin with talking points, another tool that PR pros use to help a client put his or her best foot — and voice — forward when speaking at special events, during media interviews, in conversation, during times of crises and more.

Purpose

Whereas speeches provide execs with a word-for-word road map for taking part in formal speaking engagements, *talking points*, also called *speaking points*, are designed to help the client use consistent and brand-friendly messaging during events, interviews, live broadcasts, news conferences, meetings and other think-on-your-feet type situations.

When time is of the essence — for example, during a live, three-minute TV segment — talking points can also help clients remain focused in order to strategically communicate the most important messaging on behalf of their organizations.

For example, let's say you are the publicist for a celebrity chef who is publishing a new cookbook called *Holiday Eats & Sweets*. You've secured an opportunity for the chef to appear on a live cooking segment for a national news show. During the segment, the chef will be baking one of the featured holiday desserts and will be chatting with the host of the segment about the upcoming release of the cookbook.

While you certainly want your client to captivate viewers with her tips and tricks for baking the perfect white chocolate peppermint bark, you also don't want her to spend the entire two minutes so engaged in the cooking aspect of the segment that she walks away from it without accomplishing the main objective: promoting the cookbook.

Pre-interview prep with a solid set of talking points can make all the difference by familiarizing the client with important pieces of information, such as the book's release date, where viewers can purchase it or pre-order it, other featured recipes fans can look forward to, and the like.

Keeping a client on message is also crucial during times of crisis.

Often, talking points are developed to ensure that consistent messages are delivered when organizations deal with difficult decisions and situations. For example, to explain a decision to implement lay-offs, talking points are crafted and provided to senior executives and others who communicate this news to stakeholders. These talking points are core messages that a company wants to repeat and deliver in the same way, using the same language, to help people understand why lay-offs are happening and to justify the company's course of action.

(Zappala & Carden, 2010, p. 200)

While staying on message is key during interviews, crises, news conferences and other media events, it's important to note that remaining on message does *not* mean memorizing and regurgitating facts. Your client should sound like a robot and should not be a talking head rattling off facts and figures.

Instead, talking points should be used as a communications tool to prepare people within your organization to speak clearly, confidently and consistently about their brand in a way that is natural, conversational and true to them.

Public relations pros are not only tasked with creating talking points but also updating them regularly to ensure that execs have the most up-to-date information about their organizations.

The job doesn't stop there, however, as simply having talking points on hand does not guarantee a successful interview or speaking engagement. PR pros must meet with their clients regularly to review speaking points to ensure they are confident with the material. Many times, this involves a mock interview in which the PR person plays the role of the interviewer and asks the client anticipated questions. Designating time to review speaking points also gives the client an opportunity to ask any questions he or she may have about the material, the event or media opportunity, proper dress attire and any other needed preparations.

❖ WHAT IS A RUN-OF-SHOW?

Along with talking points and shot lists (up next in Chapter 18), public relations pros working with events are often responsible for creating, contributing to and/or managing what is called a run of show. A run of show is a document that contains a detailed timeline of an event from start to finish that includes key players and specifies who is responsible for what.

From setup to breakdown and all the minutiae in between, it provides a minute-by-minute rundown of all event activities, whether it be when guests arrive, when the second course is served, when a speaker starts and finishes, or when the last song is played. A run of show is shared with event staff, security, vendors, performers, speakers, the venue and anyone who has a stake in the success of your event.

While it's not writing in the traditional sense, creating a run of show is certainly just as much work, as it involves collaborating with multiple departments and entities. A standard run of show is formatted as a spreadsheet or a table with columns labeled "Time," "Activity," "Responsibility" and "Notes" (in that order), however, these labels can also be collapsed to simply include "Time" and "Comments" or "Time" and "Activity."

For example:

Time	Activity
4:15 p.m.	Valet service begins at porte cochère (Contact: Eric Edmonds with Security.)
5–5:30 p.m.	Cocktail hour begins outside Ballroom 1. Bar tenders begin service and canapés are served (Contact: Nancy Waters with Catering).
5:30–6 p.m.	Doors to Ballroom 1 open. Guests are seated. Bars begin service inside.
6 p.m.–6:15 p.m.	Opening Remarks from president & CEO Richard Walkins (Contact: Joe Sterling with Public Relations)

And, so on ...

A well-written run-of-show ensures that everyone is on the same page and that everyone is held accountable, so that when — not if — something doesn't go according to plan, you, as the PR contact, can step in and communicate as appropriate. As they say, the show must go on.

Format

Similar to most forms of public relations writing, talking points may be formatted in different ways depending on organizational style and/or the specific purpose of the talking points. General talking points kept on file about a brand may be broken down using various subheads that together provide an overview of an organization through basic facts and figures. Talking points created for a specific event or interview, on the other hand, might be formatted using a Q&A style.

While one set of talking points may look different than the next, something they all have in common is that, like fact sheets, they communicate information using bullet points. Talking points are typically written in full sentences, although phrases and words may also be used, for example, when coaching a new president and CEO on certain buzzwords to use when speaking about his or her university. The subhead might read "Core Values" and could be followed by bulleted words and phrases such as "mission-driven," "student-centered," "research-intensive," "academic excellence," "innovation," "experiential learning," etc.

Structure

Regardless of their contents, talking points documents should be structured the same using the below elements.

Header

The header area of talking points should contain the organization's official logo, the logo for one of its entities/departments, or a special event logo created by the organization. The logo used should speak to the subject matter. For example, if you're crafting talking points for the chef of a restaurant that's owned and operated by the hotel, use the restaurant's logo rather than the hotel logo. While the chef certainly represents the hotel, as well, the restaurant's logo is more specific and reflective of the subject matter. Another option would be to include both logos.

Another instance in which you would want to include multiple logos would be an event or initiative involving a collaboration or partnership with another organization. In these cases, include their logo alongside your organization's logo. For example, let's say an organization is teaming up with The Salvation Army to host a holiday toy drive, and you've been charged with creating talking points for an exec to use during a radio interview promoting the toy drive. In this case, you'd want to include both the organization's logo and The Salvation Army's logo.

Following the logo(s), the document should include a header with the speaker's name and position, followed by a title such as "Talking Points" or "Speaking Points" that specifies the document's purpose. The title area should also clearly specify the subject matter, whether it's as broad as the organization as a whole (e.g., "The Salvation Army") or as specific as a certain event, initiative, etc. ("2018 Hope for the Holidays Toy Drive").

While general speaking points about an organization can simply feature a logo and a title, talking points created for specific individuals, events and interviews should include those details in the header area.

Speaking Points
Susan Kent, president and CEO
Ribbon Cutting Event, College of Nursing

Date: Jan. 2, 2019
Time: 10–11 a.m.
Location: Bay State University's Main Campus, Wilson Building (front entrance)

Body

As stated previously, there's a number of ways to format the body of a talking points document: subheads categorizing different topics, questions and answers (Q&A), or even just a basic running list of bullet points.

A public relations writer should select a style that will best prepare the client for the specific speaking engagement/media opportunity at hand. An exec preparing to address the media during a news conference, for instance, would best benefit from a Q&A approach.

As mentioned above, bullet points are traditionally written in full sentences. Speaking points should have a natural, conversational tone. Clients will, and should, communicate the information in their own words to avoid sounding too rehearsed or inauthentic.

Some speaking points documents will conclude with any relevant boilerplates for added information. For example, a boilerplate created for an initiative or annual event.

❖ PERSPECTIVE FROM THE PROS

By Larry Carrino

Like public relations itself, crafting solid talking points and an effective run-of-show is an art *and* a science. Go too hard in either direction and you can lose the purpose or the nuance needed behind each.

Over the years, I've written volumes of talking points that should always be conversational in tone. Talking points often fail when they are nothing more than a regurgitation of facts, which sets up a false premise for the client; that the interview he or she is giving should be, for them, nothing more than that. Getting in the facts regardless of an interview's flow shouldn't be the end game. Great interviews, even minor ones, are great conversations and talking points should be crafted as such. The biggest error is writing them as if they are to be delivered like word salad or fact bombs regardless of context. We see it all the time, the most graphic examples in political media where a compelling "one-on-one" or debate is derailed by the subject's desire to get their talking points stated instead of answering a direct question. Talking points, at their best, should be written in a clear, conversational style and, during pre-interview prep, reinforced with the following directive: "You are having a conversation. Look for opportunities to slip in the points; forcing them will appear blatantly obvious. And a talking head does not make for a compelling interview."

An ill-conceived run-of-show fails along the same lines. Truth be told, it's not an attention to detail or an abundance of facts that derails it. It's a failure to allow wiggle room within the run-of-show. We all know that hardly anything goes "according to plan." That's not to say that drafting a run-of-show is an exercise in futility. As publicists, we must be prepared, we must plan. But we must plan for things to *not* go smoothly, to not "stick to script." The best run-of-shows embrace the (controlled) chaos of an event and cover options for adjustment based on delays (read: talent not sticking to the approved timeline). If that happens, as they say, the show must go on! The question is: what do *you* do when the unexpected happens? What adjustments can be made so that the event continues seemingly without a hiccup? A well-constructed run-of-show is more than just an outline of how things should go but should have, built into it, flexibility for any contingency that might arise. Remember, sometimes even your back-up plan needs a back-up plan.

Talking Points Template

Organization's Logo(s)
Name of Speaker, Title
Speaking Points
Name of Event/Media Opportunity

Date:

Time:

Location:

<u>**Subhead or Question**</u>

- Speaking points should be written in natural, conversational tone (e.g., "We pride ourselves on," "it's *our* mission to make our customers happy," etc.).
- Continue speaking points within each subhead as needed.

<u>**Subhead or Question**</u>

- Speaking points are traditionally written in full sentences, although phrases and key words can be used, as well.
- Continue speaking points as needed.

<u>**Subhead or Question**</u>

- Continue speaking points as needed.

Optional: Include any relevant boilerplates.

Exercises

Exercise 17.1 – Talking Points

Work with a student organization or local nonprofit to identify an upcoming event the organization plans to host or participate in. Using the template provided in this chapter, create a set of talking points for the organization's spokesperson (e.g., president, VP, etc.)

that he or she can use to strategically communicate the organization's messaging for the event.

As the PR contact, you decide whether subheads or a Q&A style best communicates the information. Remember to include the organization's logo, a special event logo, and/or the logo of any organizations your "client" has partnered with for the event.

Exercise 17.2 – Run of Show

Using the same event you created talking points for above, work with the organization's contact to create a basic run of show. The run of show should detail the event — or the organization's specific involvement with the event (e.g., participating restaurant at a food festival) — from start to finish. Use the example sample run of show included with this chapter or search online for a run of show template that best suits the organization's needs.

Reference

Zappala, J.M., & Carden, A.R. (2010). *Public Relations Writing Worktext: A Practical Guide for the Profession* (3rd ed.). New York, NY: Routledge.

Chapter 18

Shot Lists and Photo Captions

Whitney Lehmann and Heidi Carr

Chapters 7 through 12 of this text introduced public relations writing tools used to tell organizations' stories through the written word, including backgrounders, fact sheets, bio sketches, and news and feature stories. The final chapter of this text will look at two tools — shot lists and photo captions — that help PR professionals tell their stories through photos and videos.

Shot Lists

Purpose

Check the job description for any public relations position, and you'll quickly find that PR pros spend a great deal of time working with organizational photography and videography. A typical day on the job might include:

- Managing an organization's photo/video budget.
- Providing rates, times and event information to photographers and videographers.
- Hiring and scheduling professional photographers to document an organization's events, execs (headshots), products/services or its property.
- Hiring and scheduling professional videographers to capture events and/or b-roll.
- Working with in house photographers and videographers on projects.
- Creating shot lists for photo/video projects and sending them to photographers and videographers in advance.
- Coordinating any necessary props for photo/video shoots.
- Escorting photographers/videographers on site during shoots.
- Directing photo/video shoots.
- Working with photographers/videographers during the editing process.
- Maintaining an organization's photo/video drives.

It should be noted that while the above tasks focus on job duties related to professional photography and videography, PR folks are also often expected to get behind the camera themselves, whether it be for event photography, social media content or other storytelling purposes.

Considering the amount of time and money that organizations spend on photography and videography, it's crucial that public relations professionals properly communicate the vision and goals for any specific project with photographers and videographers. How do they successfully communicate this information? Using shot lists.

Shot lists are documents created for specific photo and video projects that include an overview of the event/subject matter, the photo and PR contacts, the schedule, the location, key players and, most importantly, the requested shots. Hence, "shot" list.

Similar to a run of show, a shot list includes a timeline of events, but rather than specifying who's responsible for what, it specifies what shots need to happen when. Shot lists can also include photos of key players, so that photographers and videographers can easily identify them, and they can also include inspirational shots illustrating the types of shots desired.

Structure

Unlike a run of show, a shot list is not formatted as spreadsheet or table. Shot lists are structured more like talking points with a header area followed by subheads and bullet points.

Header

The header area of a shot list should contain the following elements (bold and centered):

- **Logo:** Organization's logo, special event logo, and/or logo of partner organizations.
- **Event/project:** State the name of the specific event/project (e.g., Runway Magazine Cover Party).
- **Date:** Include the day of the week, the month, day and year (e.g., Monday, Aug. 5, 2019).
- **Title:** The document's title should read "Photo Shot List" or "Video Shot List."

Body

The body of the shot list should begin with this block of information (left aligned):

Photo Contact: Name and phone number for hired photographer/videographer
PR Contact: Name and phone number(s) for PR contact(s) managing the shoot
Schedule: Include a call time (AKA arrival time) and the time frame for the actual shoot (e.g., 6–8 p.m.)
Location: Location for the photo shoot, including a full address if necessary
Overview: Provide a description of the event/project in a paragraph or less (e.g., Runway Magazine is hosting a cover party to celebrate the magazine's Spring 2020 issue featuring singer Presley Layne. More than 200 guests have been invited to the cover party featuring appetizers, cocktails, desserts and music by world-famous DJ Joe Z. Layne will perform her new single during the event.)

Next, provide a timeline using subheads that break down the window of photography (e.g., 6–8 p.m.) by requested shots. For example:

SHOT LIST

- **6–6:30 p.m. [Décor Shots/Signage]**
  - wide shot of room/décor
  - detailed shots of signature cocktails and featured appetizers
  - ice sculpture of magazine cover
  - models/servers
  - table settings/florals
- **6:30–7 p.m. [Step & Repeat]**
  - Step & Repeat shots of Presley Layne (solo)
  - Step & Repeat shots of Presley & Runway Magazine editor-in-chief Charlie Taylor
  - Step & Repeat shots of Presley & Runway Magazine publisher Sienna Lee
  - Step & Repeat shots of Presley & VIP guests
- **7–7:30 p.m. [Party Action Shots]**
  - Presley mingling with guests
  - magazine VIPs mingling
  - guests mingling with each other
  - servers passing out cocktails/appetizers
  - DJ Joe Z spinning tracks
- **7:30–7:45 p.m. [Performance]**
  - Presley Layne performs her hit single "Sideways" on main stage
  - Presley singing/dancing with backup dancers
  - Presley interacting with guests
  - guests enjoying the performance

Shot List Template

LOGO
Name of Event/Project
Date
Photo Shot List

Photo Contact: First Last, 555-555-5555
PR Contact: First Last, 555-555-5555
Schedule: Call Time: <insert time>
Photography: <insert time>
Location: Name of location (full address)
Overview: Include an overview of the event

SHOT LIST
XX – XX a.m./p.m. [Shot Description]

- list specific shots here
- shots continued

XX – XX a.m./p.m. [Shot Description]

- list specific shots here
- shots continued

XX – XX a.m./p.m. [Shot Description]
- list specific shots here
- shots continued

Photo Captions

You've hired and scheduled the photographer. You've carefully crafted a shot list. You've escorted the photographer on site for the photo shoot and spent a day, or perhaps several days, shooting, switching locations and switching locations, again. The photographer has spent the last two weeks carefully editing your images and narrowing down the hundreds of shots to a select few. Now, what do you do with them?

Purpose

Photos can be used for a variety of PR projects. They can be sent to the media (e.g., photo releases) used in advertisements, featured on an organization's website and social media, and used in company publications/newsletters.

While a photo is worth a thousand words, you're going to need a few more in order to fully tell its story. This is where photo captions come in. *Photo captions*, also known as *cutlines*, describe or explain what's taking place in a photo. They also identify the individuals in them.

Crafting Cutlines
By Heidi Carr

If a picture says 1,000 words, why do we need to write captions to go with them?

Images are often the first thing the eye goes to, making photos just as important, if not more important, as the news releases, story pitches and features they accompany.

And the caption that goes with a photo can draw a reader in – or turn them away.

But yet they are often treated as an afterthought.

Let's go over some guidelines on what all photo captions must include, and then we'll work on making those captions have an impact.

Three Basic Kinds of Photos

Mugshots: These are headshots of one person. These would never run alone. They are usually ½ column or 1 column wide. If the photo is being indented into the body copy, just use the person's last name. (Of course, the person must be named fully in the story).

Standalone photos: Also called "Wild Art" and "Day Shots," these photos do not accompany a story, hence the name. When writing a standalone caption, or cutline as they are also called, you should remember there is no other information being given, so these captions tend to be longer.

Photos that run with a story: They may show a person or people, an item (think of those food photos you post on Instagram all the time), or a landscape. They are usually recent photos, although there are times when a file photo is used. This should be indicated in the caption. More on this later.

Basic Rules

All photos require captions.

You would never send something out with an image that was not clearly identified.

When writing the caption, always have the photo in front of you.

There are many reasons for this — accuracy for one. If there are three people prominently featured in the photograph, you need to make sure you give the names for all three, and make sure the reader knows who is who. You can't do this from memory and not make a mistake at some point.

Also, I find when I'm writing a caption for a standalone photo, I need to have the image right in front of me for inspiration. It needs to talk to me.

Captions should be written in the present tense.

This creates a sense of immediacy and will have a stronger impact on the viewer.

It's OK to use quotes.

If you're using a headshot or mug of a person, you may want to give a quote or partial quote if it is very strong.

Example:

Caroline De La Rosa: 'I paint what my soul sees.'

Note that when using a quote in a caption, single quote marks are used.

Identify who is who.

When you have a row of people in your photo, identify them from left to right.

Example:

From left, Washington & Lee seniors Sofia Abdullah, Lina Estevez and Nate Purnell are leading an initiative to ban plastic straws from use on campus.

It's fine to use something descriptive in the photo to help identify a particular person.

Example:

Alexis Reyes, wearing No. 22, high-fives teammates after winning their 13th straight game.

If the people in the photo are famous, there is no need to identify them by description or directional.

Example:

Los Angeles Sparks Forward Nneka Ogwumike shares some shooting tips with 13-year-old Samantha Derrenbacher during Tuesday's clinic at the Boys & Girls Club Summer Camp. (Ogwumike is a well-known person and her image may be familiar to many. Also, it should be apparent to the reader that one person in the photo is an adult and the other a teen who would be too young to be a professional basketball player.)

If it is a group photo, but you only need to identify one person, that's OK. Just make sure it's clear where the person you need to identify is in the photo.

Example:

Veronica Taintor, second row far right in this University of California-Los Angeles team photo, is expected to make the U.S. Olympic swim team in 2020.

Treat your captions with the same level of carefulness you would use on any other piece of writing.

Make sure the names are spelled correctly, that dates and places are correct. Then double check.

Don't repeat information in the headline.

Think of the caption as a second chance to grab the reader's attention.

Avoid the obvious.

Have you ever looked at a photo, and it's told you nothing you couldn't see for yourself?

Here are some examples:

Wrong: Amanda Mountcastle holds her college diploma.

Duh, people can see there is a woman and she is holding her diploma. Use this opportunity to give a bit of information that is in the story running with the photo.

Right: Amanda Mountcastle, who graduated summa cum laude with a degree in public relations, created a website to help students find summer internships.

If you've written a caption that reads, "Amanda smiles (or sits, or waves, or cries)," you've written the obvious. And that's boring.

Words to avoid

"Is pictured," "poses," "is shown," "looks on."

Right: Gabrielle L'Hussier created her prom dress with $15 of purple tulle and acrylic paint.

Wrong: Gabrielle L'Hussier poses with the prom dress she designed.

Don't editorialize.

Don't assume a person is unhappy just because they aren't smiling. It's hard to know how a person really feels from looking at a photo. Unless they have told the photographer and writer that they are angry, impatient or lucky, don't write that they are.

Don't tell the reader or viewer that the photo is beautiful …

… Or unique or scary. Give the facts that are known and let the reader come to their own conclusion.

Keep the tone right.

If your photo and story are serious, then keep your caption serious, too. Never write something that is ironic or funny when the situation is sensitive.

If the topic is lighthearted, then let the caption match that sentiment. You want the headline, photo and story content to work together as a package.

Keep captions short.

Think of it as a tease to read the accompanying article.

Keep it conversational.

Write it like you were talking to a friend.

Now let's move on to a few special circumstances. Let's talk about file photos and photos that come from a service.

Timing

If the event happened less than a week ago, give the day (i.e. Monday, Tuesday…).

Example: Sidney Auerbach reads excerpts from his new mystery novel at City Lights bookstore Books & Books during a book-signing event Sunday night.

If the event happened within the last year, give the month.

Example: Organizers say participants in the October Walk to End Alzheimer's event in Athens, Georgia, raised more than $4 million.

If the event happened a previous year, give the year.

Example: More than 500,000 people attended the 2019 ZestFest, the annual Houston festival that features the spiciest food from around the nation.

File photos

If it's a file photo, you must include the time period the photo was taken. For example, if there is a reason to include a photo of New York City prior to 9/11, then you should note that it is a file photo. Remember, the city has a vastly different skyline now than it did 20 years ago.

Sometimes using file photos are necessary, such as if you're trying to show a design style from the 1920s or if your article is based on historical information.

Let's say, for example, you are writing a promotional piece for an event commemorating the 50th anniversary of the moon landing. You would want to include the year, and possibly the exact date if that is relevant.

Note: Remember to set off years in commas when you are giving a specific date.

Example:

Right: When Neil Armstrong put his left foot on the lunar surface the night of July 20, 1969, he said, "That's one small step for man, one giant leap for mankind."

Wrong: When Neil Armstrong put his left foot on the lunar surface the night of July 20, 1969 he said, "That's one small step for man, one giant leap for mankind."

Credit

Always make sure you have the right to send out or publish the photo. And always give the organization or wire service credit.

Example: Courtesy of The Smithsonian Institution

Multiple Photos

When running more than one photo, always identify which image the caption goes with.

Example: Let's say we have two photos in this package. One is a long hallway with dozens of people lined up holding sheet music. The other is a close up shot of a young woman with one arm in the air and the other holding a microphone. Identify the young woman with a directional:

Thousands of want-to-be "American Idol" contestants take part in the two-day tryouts in Atlanta. Below, Gabi Sterling, a 21-year old Georgia Tech student, belts out a rousing rendition of "Don't Rain on My Parade" for her audition piece.

Practice

Now let's take what you've just learned and put it into practice. I'm going to give you two scenarios for each of the photos below. Write a caption to go with the image based on the different pieces of information you are given. Unless otherwise noted, assume these are captions running with photos that have a story (or news release) attached.

Exercise 18.1

Photo credit: © digitalskillet1 - stock.adobe.com

Figure 18.1

<u>Scenario 1:</u> Trea Fisher has been named CEO of the Frontpage Media Group. She is the first black female to lead the 150-year old media company. She was previously the dean at Southwestern University's School of Communication. Her advice to women in business: "Always envision where you want to go and find people who can help you get there."

<u>Scenario 2:</u> This is a file photo of Trea Fisher, taken the day she opened her cupcake shop, Trea's Treats, in October 2002. The business has expanded, and there are now more than 150 bakeries in 40 states across the country. This is to run with a news release that Fisher's company has just been sold for more than $80 million to Martha Stewart.

Exercise 18.2

Photo credit: © vectorfusionart - stock.adobe.com

Figure 18.2

Scenario 1: The Spokane Medical Center is sponsoring a 5K the morning of June 1. Runners and walkers are invited to participate. It's part of a health fair targeted at women. Prizes will be awarded to the women who finish first in the following age groups: 29 and younger; 30–39; 40–49; 50–59; 60–69, and 70 and older.

Scenario 2: Alicia Ivaldi not only raced in the San Antonio, Texas, marathon, she did so just three weeks after giving birth. Ivaldi is wearing tag No. 1652. She runs at least one marathon a year but didn't expect to compete in this one. Her husband and newborn daughter were on the sidelines cheering her on. She finished the course at an impressive 5:01:40.

Exercise 18.3

Photo credit: © Angelov - stock.adobe.com

Figure 18.3

Scenario 1: The first day of Poetry Month at Poplar Forest Elementary kicked off with 5-year-old Amalia Harris writing a poem about her dog, Sparky. The first day was Wednesday, April 1, and throughout the month, students at the school will be reading and writing poetry.

Write this one to be a standalone caption.

Scenario 2: In order to encourage students to read, the Evanston City Library is encouraging children to read aloud to their pets. The animals are non-judgmental, and it helps build the child's confidence. "They're not going to correct the child if she mispronounces a word," said librarian Sabrina Ortiz.

Exercise 18.4

Photo credit: © Mongkolchon - stock.adobe.com

Figure 18.4

Scenario 1: Alexander Piacentino has been named manager of the year by National Technologies. Alex is the man with the beard. He is being handed a certificate of excellence by his boss, Michael Kamphorst, during an awards ceremony at the corporation's Charlotte, North Carolina, headquarters. Piancentino was given the award for his innovations in energy efficiency.

Scenario 2: You are promoting an online technology program where students can take a number of specific courses. Graduates of the program are promised they will find higher-paying jobs in their field or receive awards and commendations after completing the program. This is a stock photo to accompany the news release.

Exercise 18.5

Photo credit: © saksit - stock.adobe.com

Figure 18.5

Scenario 1: You are representing a company that promises to help college students find the best jobs in the tech industry after graduation. The students who sign up with this company will have their resumes sent to the highest paying firms. The company also offers resume and interview special training. This is a generic file photo to go with the news release to announce this new program.

Scenario 2: The following students were chosen from more than 5,000 applicants for Google Scholarships. They'll each receive $50,000 and a trip to Google headquarters. The winners are Monty Li, of Massachusetts Institute of Technology; Jiaying Purnell, of Stanford University; Amy Amaya, of Carnegie Mellon University and Emely Hilliard, of Cornell University.

Exercises

Exercise 18.1 – Shot Lists

Think of an event that you recently attended, be it a movie premier, a birthday party, a baby shower, a graduation, a fundraiser, etc. Using the shot list template introduced in this chapter, craft a shot list for the event, as if you were in charge of managing photography for the event.

Use the actual date, time and location for the event. List your name as the PR contact. Improvise details where needed. For the photo contact, research a local photographer that specializes in event photography and include his or her information as if you hired him/her for the job.

Exercise 18.2 – Photo Captions

Craft a cutline for each of the five images presented in the practice section of this chapter (Exercise 18.1–18.5). Make sure to follow the "Basic Rules" outlined in this section. Base each caption on the information presented in the scenarios. Assume these are captions running with photos that have a story (or news release) attached, unless otherwise noted.

Write a memo to your instructor that includes your photo captions for Exercise 18.1– 18.5. Use today's date and "Photo Caption Exercise" as the subject. Print the memo and initial next to your name.

Afterword

Whitney Lehmann

You've made it! You've journeyed through the 18 chapters in this text and the various forms of public relations writing presented in its pages. Whether you were new to the field of public relations or a PR pro brushing up on some of the basics, my hope for you — and all users of this text — Is that you will be able to proceed with a newfound confidence when approaching all types of PR writing. Whether you're writing a cover letter for your dream job, crafting a news release for a client, sprucing up your bio, penning a simple thank you note, or engaging in any other type of PR writing in your personal or professional life, I hope you'll reach for this text.

You will find that you can apply the core principles of PR writing to just about any form of the written — and even spoken — word. The inverted pyramid can be applied to conversations, too!

The work doesn't, and shouldn't, stop here, however. Although the principles of public relations writing will not change, the channels we use to communicate will continue to evolve and we, as PR practitioners, need to evolve along with them. Below, I've offered some suggestions for how we can continue to develop as PR writers and practitioners while building upon the principles explored in this text:

- *Current Events* – Commit to current events by consuming multiple sources of hyperlocal, local, national and international news. Whether you read, watch or listen to the news, what's most important is that you are consuming it on a daily basis and becoming a connoisseur of current events. Being tapped into the news is part of the job description.
- *Associated Press Stylebook* – As mentioned in Chapter 1, the Associated Press publishes an updated print edition of the AP Stylebook each spring and updates its digital version regularly. Whether you use it in print or digital form, it's important to stay abreast of any changes from year to year. Commit to getting, and using, the new edition each year. Don't forget to check out the "What's new" section at the front of the book for any major updates to AP Style.
- *Industry Sources* – Stay tapped into industry news by following industry sources, such as *PR Daily*, *PR News*, publications from the Public Relations Society of America, such as *Strategies and Tactics*, and more.

Student Opportunities:

- *Public Relations Student Society of America (PRSSA)*
- *PRSA Certificate in Public Relations*

Professional Opportunities:

- *Public Relations Society of America (PRSA)*
- *Accreditation in Public Relations (APR) through the Universal Accreditation Board (UAB)*

Visit prsa.org or prssa.prsa.org to learn how you can get involved in your local PRSA and PRSSA chapters.

Index